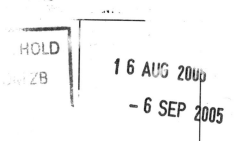

ORIENT LINE

A FLEET HISTORY

PAR·NON·LEONINA·SOCIETAS

ORIENT CRUISES

Managers: Anderson Green & Co.,Ltd. 5,Fenchurch Avenue,E.C.3.

CONVENIENT TRAINS FROM ALL STATIONS ON THE LMS IN CONNECTION WITH THESE SAILINGS

ORIENT LINE

A FLEET HISTORY

Peter Newall

Ships in Focus Publications

Published in the UK in 2004 by Ships in Focus Publications,
18 Franklands, Longton
Preston PR4 5PD

© 2004 Peter Newall and Ships in Focus Publications
Designed by John Clarkson

Printed by Amadeus Press Ltd., Cleckheaton.
Typeset by Highlight Type Bureau, Bradford
ISBN 1 901703 46 0

Left: 1930s Orient Line cruise poster by Andrew Johnson. *[Christie's Images Ltd.]*
Cover: *Oriana's* funnel and *Orontes* (2) leaving Cape Town in 1961. *[P&O; Ian Shiffman]*
Back cover upper: *Orsova* (1) departing Sydney Heads. By John C. Allcot (1888-1973), signed and dated 1921.
[Courtesy of The British Mercantile Marine Memorial Collection.]
Back cover lower: *Orion. [V.H. Young and L.A. Sawyer collection]*

*This book is dedicated to all
those who served with Orient Line
and its predecessors*

Orient (2) painted by W.L. Wyllie (1851-1931).

4

CONTENTS

Austral entering the Thames. By R.H. Neville Cumming (1843-1920), signed and dated 1889.
[Courtesy of The British Mercantile Marine Memorial Collection.]

FOREWORD

When asked how my career in travel and transport began, I tell people the simple truth. I ran away to sea.

It might not have been a gesture of high melodrama as the notion suggests, but it was the result of ambition to get away from the deprivations of immediate post-war Britain and experience the wider world. To find oneself duly signed on as a Cadet Purser by the great Orient Line was a distinct bonus and source of some pride.

Sailing aboard *Orcades, Orion, Oronsay, Orsova* and *Otranto* on the long deep-sea routes down to Australia and across the Pacific to the USA was a dream come true for a young man of the drab 1950s. The work was hard and the passengers - especially the emigrant families - demanding, but I have been forever grateful for the way Orient Line taught me the disciplines of teamwork, leadership and the art of good customer service.

The sense of history that comes from witnessing the timeless bustle of port activity at Tilbury, Colombo, Fremantle or San Francisco or from practising the ancient customs of life at sea, is profound. I was ever aware of the legacy we inherited from predecessor seafarers and famous old vessels, all the way back to the original *Orient* of 100 years before.

In turn, I now look back to my time at sea and realise just how much today's burgeoning international air transport industry owes to the great shipping lines of the last century.

I am grateful to my former British Airways colleague, Peter Newall, for his dedication to recording the definitive history of Orient Line. He has conserved a rich heritage.

Lord Marshall of Knightsbridge
Chairman, British Airways

INTRODUCTION

For over 100 years, Orient Line was one of the most progressive and innovative of all British shipping lines. Its success was due almost entirely to the extraordinary leadership of the Anderson family who, despite numerous setbacks, managed to keep control of the business right up to the end. Following the example set by its founder James Anderson, the running of Orient was shared by family members with none of the dominance of a single individual which brought about the early demise of other shipping companies.

Because of the Anderson connection, this history of Orient Line starts in 1863 when the London firm of loading agents, of which James Anderson was a partner, was renamed Anderson, Thomson and Company. By then it operated a fleet of sailing ships primarily to the West Indies and Australia including *Orient* which gave the company its "Orient" Line of Clipper Ships name. The strong link with the Australian trade also led to the formation of The Orient Steam Navigation Company in 1878.

For the first twenty-five years of its existence The Orient Steam Navigation Company was closely associated with the Pacific Steam Navigation Company (P.S.N.C.) and the two operated a joint service to Australia under the Orient Line banner. For some reason, the P.S.N.C. ships, many of which were built specially for the trade, have been excluded from some of the earlier Orient Line histories. All these ships are featured in this book.

With the loss of Orient Line's records during the London Blitz, the early history of the company has been difficult to piece together and I am extremely grateful to P&O's Historian and Archivist, Stephen Rabson, for his generous help with access to the P&O archives, most of which are held by the National Maritime Museum at Greenwich. Stephen also helped unravel some of the key events in the company's history. For the history of the individual ships I have been given great assistance from a number of friends and colleagues and I would also like to offer special thanks to Andrew Bell, Roy Fenton, Fred Hawks, Bill Laxon, John Naylon and Bill Schell.

Lord Marshall of Knightsbridge very kindly agreed to write the foreword and I am sure that many readers will be pleasantly surprised to see that his career started with Orient Line. His leadership during my time at British Airways was inspiring and he has served as a rôle model ever since.

I would also like to thank my publishers for their faith in this project and their quest to find the best possible photographs, most of which have never been published before.

Many thanks for photographs and information to: Dag Bakka, Declan Barriskill, David Burrell, John Clarkson, James Cooper, Anne Cowne, Jill Davies, Andrew Davis, Ian Farquhar, Heather Fenton, Ambrose Greenway, Valerie Hart, David Hodge, Barbara Jones, Bård Kolltveit, John Landels, Martin Lindenborn, Louis Loughran, Paul Louden-Brown, Martin McIlwrath, David Mearns, Robert Pabst, Nicholas Pusenjak, Stuart Rankin, Lisa Royall, Ian Shiffman, Shane Spencer, Helen Trepa and David Whiteside. If I have left anyone out, please accept my apologies.

Peter Newall, Blandford Forum
June 2004

NOTES ON THE FLEET LISTS

Fleet lists are presented in the format used in the publisher's *Record,* and which is adapted from that developed and refined by the World Ship Society. This format has the merits of being concise, familiar, and flexible.

The fleet lists are divided as follows: Anderson, Thomson and Co. after 1st January 1863 (Anderson, Anderson and Co. from December 1869); Orient Line Joint Service 1878-1909; Orient Steam Navigation Co. Ltd. 1909-1966; Orient Steam Navigation Co. Ltd. (P&O Bulk Shipping Division, managers) liquid gas and ore/bulk/oil carriers 1977-1987; post First World War managed ships 1919-1921; Second World War managed ships.

All the ships are listed in chronological order according to registration or management dates or, in the case of some of the P.S.N.C. ships, when they entered the joint service. The only exceptions to the chronological sequence are the early P.S.N.C. ships, which were transferred to the Australian route or bought by Orient Line. For greater clarity, these have been grouped together at the start of the Orient Line Joint Service fleet list.

The numeral in brackets following the name of a ship indicates if the ship was the first, second etc. with that name in the fleet. If a numeral is not given, it was the only one with that name. The ship's name is followed by the period in which it was in the fleet or on the joint service with P.S.N.C. Next is indicated the hull material, number of screws if more than one and, for sailing vessels, the rig. Ships not otherwise described are steel steamers or motor vessels.

On the first line is the official number (O.N.) which is allocated to a British ship when first registered. This numbering system applied throughout the British Empire and Commonwealth and remained with the ship whenever it was British Empire and Commonwealth registered. In 'Lloyd's Register' and the 'Mercantile Navy List', the official number for the ship is always shown in the first column. The registered tonnages, gross (g) and net (n), and dimensions in feet (length x breadth x draft) are those at the time of completion. Registered length is between perpendiculars except for the liquid gas and ore/bulk/oil carriers 1977-1987 which are shown with length overall and dimensions in metres.

On the following line is a description of the engine(s) fitted and the name of their builder. Steam engines may be single cylinder (1-cyl.), two cylinder compounds (C. 2-cyl.), three or four cylinder triple expansion (T. 3-cyl. or T. 4-cyl.), or quadruple expansion four cylinder (Q. 4-cyl.). For oil engines are given the type (e.g. Sulzer, Burmeister & Wain), the number of cylinders, whether two stroke (2SC) or four stroke (4SC) cycle, single acting (SA) or double acting (DA). Various figures for horsepower are given: nominal (NHP), indicated (IHP), or shaft (SHP) for turbines. Nominal horsepower bears least relationship to the engine's actual power, but is often the only figure available. The speed is taken from registration documents or 'Lloyd's Register', and is usually an estimate not a trial's figure. The speeds shown also tend to be service speeds or best averages when the engines were relatively new, and during fair weather conditions. Any changes of engine are listed, with dates, on subsequent lines.

Passenger numbers can also vary considerably and where they are included they are usually when the ship was completed, followed by any major changes which occurred.

Apart from a few of the more recent ships, the key details for each ship under British ownership have been obtained from the registration documents in classes BT107-110 at the National Archives, Kew.

SOURCES

Primary sources
Board of Trade Casualty Returns
Bureau Veritas
Lloyd's Register of Shipping
Lloyd's Register Wreck Books
Lloyd's War Losses - World War One
Lloyd's War Losses - World War Two
Lloyd's List
Lloyd's Shipping Index
Lloyd's Confidential Index
Lloyd's Weekly Casualty Reports
Marine News
Mercantile Navy List
Orient Line press cuttings: National Maritime Museum, Greenwich
Orient Guide 1888, 1889 and 1901
Rhodes Directory of Passenger Steamers
Sea Breezes
Shipbuilding & Shipping Record
The Journal of Commerce
The Shipbuilder & Marine Engine-builder
White papers on Boer War Transport movements
World War One Service List
World War Two Ministry of War Transport Service List

Other sources
Green, E and Moss, M. *A Business of National Importance - the Royal Mail Shipping Group, 1902-1937.* Methuen, London, 1982
Isherwood, JH and Stewart, Colin. *Ships of the Orient Line,* Adlard Coles, Southampton, c. 1954
Kludas, A and Bischoff, H. *Die Schiffe der Hamburg-Amerika Linie 1847-1970,* Koehlers, Herford, 1979
Kludas, A. *Die Seeschiffe des Norddeutschen Lloyd 1920-1970,* Koehlers, Herford, 1992

Kludas A., Cooper, James and Pein, Joachim. *The Hamburg South America Line,* World Ship Society, Kendal, 1989
Lesslie, RJ. The Firm: unpublished history of Anderson, Green and Co. Ltd. and its predecessors written in the 1920s, P&O archives
Maber, JM. *North Star to Southern Cross,* T. Stephenson and Sons, Prescot, 1967
McCart, Neil. *Passenger Ships of the Orient Line,* Patrick Stephens, Cambridge, 1987
McCarthy, Mike. *Jervoise Bay Shipwrecks,* Western Australian Museum, 1992
Marshall, Gordon de L. *Memories of Maritime Albany,* Western Australian Maritime Museum, 1991.
Mitchell, WH and Sawyer, LA. *The Liberty Ships,* Lloyd's of London Press, London, 1985
Morris, Charles F. *Origins, Orient and Oriana,* Toredo Books, Brighton, 1980
Orient Line Australian Annals, 1946. Unpublished history of Orient Line in Australia.
Ormston, John M. *The Five Minute Crossing,* Thurrock Local History Society, 1988.
Rabson, S. and O'Donoghue, K. *P&O, A Fleet History,* World Ship Society, Kendal, 1988
Rankin, S. *Shipbuilding in Rotherhithe - Greenland Dock & Barnard's Wharf,* Dockside Studio, London, 1999
Spindler, Rear Adm. *Der Krieg zur See: Der Handelskrieg mit U-booten, Volumes 1 to 5,* Mittler & Sons, Berlin, 1932-1966
Tennent, AJ. *British Merchant Ships sunk by U-boats in the 1914-1918 War,* AJ Tennent, Chipstead, Kent, 1990
Turner, M. *Shipwrecks and Salvage in South Africa - 1505 to the present,* C. Struik, 1988
A Voyage with the Mails, circa 1910-1914. Orient Line souvenir book for passengers

THE EARLY YEARS:
ANDERSON, ANDERSON AND CO.

The Anderson connection
The Anderson family played a pivotal role in the evolution of Orient Line. No relation of P&O's founder, Arthur Anderson, James Anderson was born at Peterhead in Aberdeenshire in 1811. Following the death of his doctor father in 1812, James was brought up by his mother and in 1828 he joined the London shipping firm, James Thomson and Co., founded in 1797. The company, based at 6 Billiter Square, had its own fleet of sailing ships and was also a leading loading agent and insurance broker.

In 1841 James Anderson was made a partner of James Thomson and Co. and by the time the firm was renamed Anderson, Thomson and Co. in 1863 he had become the prime mover in the company. James was joined by other members of the Anderson family and, when the last of the Thomsons retired, Anderson, Anderson and Co. was formed at the end of December 1869. In the meantime, in 1861, the company moved its office to nearby 1 Billiter Court.

West Indies trade
Much of the company's business was in the West Indies, especially Jamaica. As well as being the outward-loading agents for Cottam, Mortan and Co. and Thomas Hankey and Co., Anderson also had a sizeable fleet of sailing ships, mainly barques, which carried an assortment of cargoes from the Caribbean to London's West India Import Dock. The Jamaican products were mainly rum, pimentos, logwood, coconuts and sugar and these were transported to the ship's side by small sailing barges called droghers which were owned by the firm. Due to the lack of navigation aids in the West Indies, ship's safety was also a major problem in the mid-nineteenth century and many of the Anderson sailing ships were wrecked.

James Anderson, 1811-1896

With the increased production of beet sugar in Europe and greater export of cane sugar from Jamaica to the United States, the Jamaica sugar trade to London declined sharply in the 1870s and in 1882 Andersons withdrew the sailing ships and substituted them with steamships. Two steamships were built for the trade, *Carib* and *Maroon*, whilst a pair of sailing ships were converted into steam-driven droghers based in Jamaica. *Maroon* was fitted with cold-air machinery, and was one of the first ships to carry bananas in bulk from the West Indies to Britain. Despite this, the West Indies business ceased in 1895.

West Coast of the Americas
In the 1850s, James Thomson and Co. obtained a large tract of land near Alberni on Vancouver Island and built a sawmill to produce spars and masts for ships. After initial success, the timber business folded although the company continued to be involved in the sailing ship trade to Vancouver until 1903 when they were unable to compete with Alfred Holt and Co.'s steamers. The company also operated to San Francisco from the early 1860s until 1893 and to Callao and Valparaiso between 1869 and 1899.

In 1871 a syndicate of London and Bremen businessmen purchased one of the greatest copper-mining centres in the world at Minas de Rio Tinto, a mining town in south west Spain. Four years later, Anderson, Anderson and Co. became the chartering brokers for the new concern, Rio Tinto Ltd. They also managed the steamers which brought supplies for the mines to the nearest port, Huelva, and loaded copper ore for the return voyage. Although the ship management contract ceased in 1884, the company remained Rio Tinto's chartering brokers well into the twentieth century.

Thomas Bilbe and Company
Thomas Bilbe (1803-1884) was a highly skilled shipwright who managed a shipyard at the Nelson Dock, Rotherhithe for Thomas King. In 1848 King sold the business to Thomas Bilbe and his partner Captain William Perry (1808-1876), a retired seafarer. Perry was a friend of James Anderson, and James Thomson and Co. had a financial stake in the new company, Thomas Bilbe and Co., which also built a number of well-known ships for the firm including *Orient* (1), and the composite ships *Coonatto* and *Yatala*. The first vessel built for James Thomson and Co. by Bilbe was the 452gt *Celestial* of 1851. *Celestial*, sold in 1861, was designed for the tea trade and was Bilbe's first ship constructed using his 'radial' system of framing.

Thomas Bilbe and Co. also built ships for their own account which operated mainly in the Far East. In 1868, after an accident, Thomas Bilbe retired and in July 1875 the shipyard was sold to the Nelson Dock Company, whilst William Perry continued to manage the ships. The Nelson Dock slipway built in 1855 still exists, as does the attractive Nelson House where Captain Perry apparently lived. Perry died in 1876 and ownership of the seven Thomas Bilbe and Co. ships passed to Anderson, Anderson and Co.

Australian passenger trade
In February 1851 gold was discovered just north of Bathurst, New South Wales. This started the Australian gold rush with thousands of fortune seekers flooding the new colonies and, in the first year, the population of Victoria doubled. The company's history also became inextricably linked with the growth of the region when James Thomson and Co.'s *Charlotte Jane* (663/1848) arrived at Lyttelton, New Zealand on 16th December 1850 with the first settlers for Christchurch. In 1853, *Orient* (1) was completed at Rotherhithe and this ship, the first in the fleet over 1,000 gross tons, was ordered especially for the gold boom in Australia. Her fame was such that the company eventually became commonly known as the 'Orient' Line of Clipper Ships. In the 1860s and 1870s a number of famous sailing

The Murray. [Maritime Museum of Monterey]

Hesperus photographed in the Thames by F.C. Gould. [National Maritime Museum G644]

ships were built for the trade carrying emigrants outbound and wool on the return journey. These included the Aberdeen-built composite ships *The Murray*, *The Goolwa* and *Darra* and the three beautiful iron ships *Hesperus*, *Aurora* and *Harbinger* from the yard of Robert Steele at Greenock. Although *Aurora* was lost on her maiden voyage, *Hesperus* and *Harbinger* remained in the Anderson, Anderson and Co. fleet until their sale to Devitt and Moore in 1890, the year after James Anderson's retirement from the firm.

Anderson, Thomson and Co. was also involved with the loading of outbound cargo to Australia. Initially, they were loading agents for Budden, Bevan and Tozer but in 1866 they took over the loading themselves and started a line to Melbourne using chartered ships. In 1874 two clerks in the loading department, O.J. Trinder and J.R. Anderson, resigned to form their own company Trinder, Anderson and Co. and two years later, in conjunction with their old employers, they were awarded the contract by the Queensland Government to carry emigrants to Brisbane.

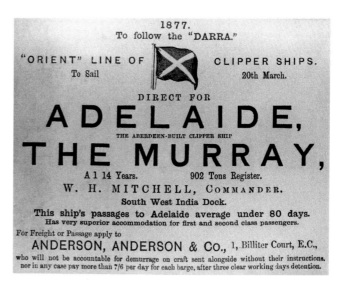

Sailing card of 1877 inviting cargo and passengers for *The Murray*
[P&O Archives]

In the early nineteenth century, the area between Leadenhall Street and Fenchurch Street was a warren of small streets including Billiter Square and Billiter Court. Much of this area was owned by the Fishmongers Company, which also had its guildhall on Fenchurch Street. James Thomson and Co. was originally based at 6 Billiter Square and in 1861 the firm, now known as Anderson, Anderson and Co., moved to 1 Billiter Court. In the late 1870s the area around Billiter Court was redeveloped and Fenchurch Avenue came into existence. New offices were built for the newly formed Orient Steam Navigation Co. Ltd. at 5 Fenchurch Avenue and these were leased from the Fishmongers Company for 80 years. This photo was taken in April 1924. Note the framed travel posters - see pages 174-175. With the destruction of its head office by German bombers in 1941, Orient Line moved to 7 Bishopsgate and returned to Fenchurch Avenue (no 14) in the 1950s. In 1960, after the integration with P&O, it relocated to 122 Leadenhall Street.
[National Maritime Museum]

As loading agents, Anderson, Anderson and Co. sent ships to all parts of the globe from London's West India Dock. Trading primarily to the West Indies, Australia, Central and South America and the west coast of North America, the company was also known as the "Orient" Line of Clipper Ships, a name taken from its famous 1853-built clipper ship *Orient*.

[P&O Archives]

THE ORIENT STEAM NAVIGATION COMPANY

Pacific Steam Navigation Company charters to Australia
The opening of the Suez Canal in 1869 and the development of more efficient steam engines had a profound impact on the shipping business to the Far East and Australasia. For the directors of Anderson, Anderson and Co., these must have been trying times as they watched other well-known sailing ship companies such as the White Star Line of Packets and the Black Ball Line of Packets go to the wall following failed attempts to switch from sail to steam. Andersons' first venture into steam was in 1874 when the steamships *Easby* (1,489/1872) and *St. Osyth* (3,541/1874) were despatched to Australia on 2nd April and 31st October respectively. These two ships were then loaded with coal at Newcastle, New South Wales for China on the triangular route to the Far East. Unfortunately the agency for this service, which became the Colonial Line, was secured by a rival London loading agent, Gellatly, Hankey and Sewell. In the mid 1870s, however, the perfect opportunity presented itself with the availability of a number of relatively new passenger ships which had been laid up by their owner, the Pacific Steam Navigation Company (P.S.N.C.).

In the late 1860s the Birkenhead-based P.S.N.C. embarked on a massive expansion programme for its services to the west coast of South America. Most of the ships were ordered from the Clyde builders John Elder and Co. John Elder had pioneered the compound engine and was also a director of P.S.N.C. and when he died in 1869, aged only 45,

the first of the new ships was named *John Elder* in his honour. By 1874, with 57 steamers, P.S.N.C. had the world's largest fleet and also the largest ship in the world (excluding the *Great Eastern*) the 4,671gt *Iberia*. Unfortunately, operating a weekly service proved too problematic and costly for P.S.N.C. and it was decided to revert to fortnightly sailings in March 1874. This meant that a large number of ships had to be laid up, including four of the *John Elder*-class ships, *Lusitania*, *Chimborazo*, *Cuzco* and *Garonne* (1).

In February 1877 Anderson, Anderson and Co. began talks with P.S.N.C. about chartering its laid-up vessels for a new monthly passenger-cargo and emigrant service between London and Australia - outbound via the Cape, returning through the Suez Canal. The partner in this new venture was another London loading agent, Frederick Green and Co. The Green family had a long association with shipbuilding on the Thames. Frederick Green's brothers Richard and Henry (R. and H. Green) owned a shipyard at Blackwall and a fleet of sailing ships and steamers. Members of the Devitt family of the famous sailing ship company Devitt and Moore were also involved in the Frederick Green and Co. business. Sir Thomas Devitt was a partner in the firm for forty years. The first ship for the new Orient Line of Steamers to Australia was *Lusitania*, which sailed from London on 26th June 1877 and arrived at Melbourne on 8th August, beating the previous record by ten days.

The first steamship chartered by Anderson and Anderson was *Easby,* which was probably on its delivery voyage to Australia having been sold by her original owners to F.C. Fulton of Dunedin, New Zealand in 1874. In 1879 she was bought by James Paterson and Co. Ltd., Melbourne and used on the Australian coal trade. On the 6th April 1907 she struck the Skerries Reef, near Point Hicks, Victoria and was abandoned. *Easby* is seen left in dry dock at Port Chalmers.

[Ian Farquhar collection]

THE ST. OSYTH, OF THE ORIENT LINE FROM LONDON TO AUSTRALIA.

An illustration of *St. Osyth* from the Illustrated London News. Note the early use of the Orient Line name.

[Peter Newall collection]

SECOND SALOON.

ORIENT LINE OF  STEAMERS TO AUSTRALIA.

NOTICE TO CABIN PASSENGERS.

1. If Cabin Passengers, through no default of their own, fail to obtain a Passage in the Ship, and on the day named in this Contract Ticket, they may obtain redress for breach of contract by summary process under the 73rd section of the "Passengers' Act, 1875."

2. Cabin Passengers must produce, on demand, their Contract Tickets to the Government Emigration Officer, under a penalty not exceeding £10. This Ticket should therefore be preserved and kept in readiness to be produced on board the Ship.

THE ORIENT STEAM NAVIGATION COMPANY'S (LIMITED) Steam-ship _Lusitania_ of _3825_ Tons Register, to sail from the Port of LONDON (GRAVESEND), for ADELAIDE, MELBOURNE AND SYDNEY, on the _twenty seventh_ day of _November_ 187_8_.

NAMES.	No. of Persons.	
	Adults above 12 Years.	Children 12 Years and under.
Mrs. I. A. Sowell _with liberty to land at Adelaide_ _Berth. 7._	1	
Total Number of Persons.	1	

In consideration of the sum of £ _36 15/—_ I hereby agree with the Persons named in the margin hereof that such Persons shall be provided with Second Saloon Class Cabin Passage in the above-named Steam Ship, to sail from the Port of London for the Port of _Sydney_ in Australia with not less than Twenty Cubical Feet of Luggage for each Person, and that such Persons shall be victualled as Second Saloon Class Cabin Passengers during the Voyage, and the Time of Detention at any Place before its Termination; and I further engage to land the Persons aforesaid, with their Luggage at the last-mentioned Port, free of any Charge beyond the Passage Money aforesaid; and I hereby acknowledge to have received the Sum of £ _18. 7. 6_ in {part} Payment of such Passage Money.

On behalf of The Orient Steam Navigation Company, Limited,

ALEXANDER GAVIN ANDERSON,

Wm Sexton

1, BILLITER COURT, LONDON, E.C.

9th Oct 187 _8_

Deposit £ _18. 7. 6_
Balance £ _18 7 6_ to be paid Three clear Days before embarking.

Total £ _36 15/—_

Received the Balance, £ _18. 7. 6_
Signature _Chas George_

19 Nov 187 _8_

N.B.—This Contract Ticket is exempt from the Stamp Duty.

All Luggage must be delivered at the South West India Dock, and the Dock Charges paid at least Three clear Days before Embarkation. The stipulations on back hereof form part of the Contract.

A passenger ticket for _Lusitania_ soon after she was bought by Orient Line. The house flag of Orient Line of Steamers was initially an amalgam of the flags of the two managers Anderson, Anderson and Co. and Frederick Green and Co. In 1880 the flag was changed to reflect the new joint service of The Orient Steam Navigation Co. Ltd. and Pacific Steam Navigation Company. _[P&O Archives]_

Formation of The Orient Steam Navigation Co. Ltd.

The success of the charters led to the formation of The Orient Steam Navigation Co. Ltd. (O.S.N.C.) on 12th February 1878 and the purchase of *Lusitania, Chimborazo, Cuzco* and *Garonne* (1). The last mentioned was also the first to fly the new Orient Line flag (a combination of the house flags of the two managing companies, Frederick Green and Co. and Anderson, Anderson and Co.) when she left London on 7th March 1878. Towards the end of that year, Orient Line agreed to operate the service jointly with P.S.N.C. and on 27th January 1879 *John Elder* made the first P.S.N.C. sailing to Australia from London. In 1879 and 1880 all the remaining Anderson sailing ships were re-registered at Aberdeen. In 1879, the newly-formed company moved to new premises at 5 Fenchurch Avenue which remained the headquarters of Orient Line until its destruction during an air raid in 1941. F. Green and Co. also had offices in Fenchurch Avenue at number 13.

Orient Line also set about ordering the first of a series of new ships. The 5,365gt *Orient* (2) was completed by John Elder and Co. in September 1879 and took the name of the famous sailing ship which had been sold in April. *Orient* (2) was the largest ship in the world after *Great Eastern* (18,915/1858) and the first to be built to Admiralty standards as an armed merchant cruiser in time of war. She was also the first passenger ship to Australia with electric light and refrigeration. With a 15-knot service speed, she broke all the existing records to Australia (London to Adelaide: 37 days 22 hours) and South Africa (Plymouth to Cape Town: 17 days 21 hours). The South African record remained unbroken for ten years.

Soon after the arrival of *Orient* (2), Orient Line and P.S.N.C. decided that, from January 1880, the joint service would be fortnightly and that the two companies would operate under the Orient Line name but with their own house flags and with Anderson, Anderson and Co. and Frederick Green and Co. acting as brokers and managers of the service. A new Orient Line flag was designed which was similar to that of P.S.N.C. with the initials O.S.N.C. Except for *Austral* of 1881, all new Orient Line passenger vessels had names beginning with the letter O whilst P.S.N.C. also adopted the same nomenclature for most of its large passenger ships.

From 1881, the new ships in both the O.S.N.C. and P.S.N.C. fleets were fitted with refrigerating machinery and Orient Line became the first shipping company to provide reefer space on the Australian trade. The carriage of frozen meat and later fruit became a significant aspect of the company operation right up to the end. Mail was also important although for the first few years the company operated without a mail subsidy. In 1883 it was awarded the New South Wales mail contract which meant an abandonment of the service via the Cape apart from the occasional extra steamer. Orient also won an emigrant contract from the New South Wales Government for £15 per head for numbers up to 400 and for £14.10s.0d. per head from 400 to 600.

Diego Garcia coaling station

Not wishing to be reliant on coal at Aden, P&O's main coaling station, in 1881 Orient and P.S.N.C. leased land at Diego Garcia in the Indian Ocean from the Mauritius Government. Each company supplied two coal hulks (Orient's were *Alchymist* (540/1859 and *Peterborough* (531/1859); P.S.N.C.'s were *Ronochan* (1,156/1849) and *Arran* (962/1851) and a jointly-owned tug, *Escort,* was built for the coaling station by R. and H. Green, Blackwall). A dozen 82-foot iron lighters were also completed in February 1882. In 1888 it was agreed that the Australian mail contract be shared between Orient Line and P&O. This stipulated a call at Colombo and the Diego Garcia coaling station was sold to William Lund and Son in December 1888. The tug *Escort* was transferred to Albany, Western Australia where she operated for the company until 1900 when the Western Australia port of call was moved from Albany to the new deep-water port at Fremantle.

Orient (2) in the Suez Canal, probably in the 1880s. *[Ambrose Greenway collection]*

ORIENT LINE

FORTNIGHTLY MAIL SERVICE

BETWEEN

ENGLAND & AUSTRALIA.

	Tons Reg.	H.P.
AUSTRAL,	5524	7000
CUZCO ...	3898	4000
GARONNE	3876	3000
IBERIA ...	4661	4200
LIGURIA ...	4648	4200

	Tons Reg.	H.P.
LUSITANIA,	3877	4000
ORIENT ...	5365	6000
ORIZABA...	6077	7000
ORMUZ ...	6031	8500
OROYA ...	6057	7000

CALLING TO LAND AND EMBARK PASSENGERS AT

GIBRALTAR, NAPLES, PORT SAID, ISMAILIA, SUEZ, COLOMBO, ALBANY, ADELAIDE, MELBOURNE & SYDNEY.

Steamers among the largest and fastest afloat, cuisine of the first order, electric lighting, hot and cold baths, good ventilation, and every comfort.

CHEAP SINGLE AND RETURN TICKETS.

Managers : { F. GREEN & Co., 13, FENCHURCH AVENUE,
{ ANDERSON, ANDERSON & Co., 5, FENCHURCH AVENUE,
LONDON, E.C.

For Passage apply to the latter Firm.

An Orient Line handbill of the late 1880s. *[P&O Archives]*

THE STEAM-SHIP ORIENT.

This magnificent new vessel arrived at the South West India Dock, from the Clyde, on the 13th ult. She has been visited by thousands of people desiring to see the finest and best-fitted ship, indeed, the only full-powered steamer expressly built and equipped for the Australian trade, and the grandest vessel for the conveyance of passengers that has ever appeared in the Thames. The Orient Steam Navigation Company, of which Messrs. F. Green and Co. and Messrs. Anderson, Anderson, and Co. are joint managers, have arranged for a line of first-class steam-ships to go out from London to Adelaide, Melbourne, and Sydney, steaming all the way in less than forty days, and to return by way of the Suez Canal. This is an entirely novel idea, as the Great Britain and other vessels, using steam, at least for auxiliary power, on the voyage out, have made the home voyage hitherto by the lengthened and inconvenient route of Cape Horn. The Orient is the first steam-ship that has been constructed expressly for the new service. She is, after the Great Eastern, which is said to roll too much for passengers' use, all but the largest of existing merchant steam-ships ; only the Inman steam-ship City of Berlin, the Britannic and Germanic, of the White Star line, and the Arizona, of the Guion line, can in size at all bear comparison with her. The displacement weight of the Orient is 9500 tons ; her registered tonnage is 5400 tons; her length is 460 ft.; her beam, 46·35 ft., her depth to main deck 27·1 ft. ; to upper deck 35·1 ft. When she takes her place on the service of the direct Orient line to Australia for which she has been built, the Orient will be prepared to carry, in addition to 3000 tons of Welsh coal (more than sufficient to take her to Australia), 3600 tons of measurement cargo, which might weigh 1000 tons or so. She would also carry 120 first-class passengers, 130 second-class, and 300 third-class or steerage passengers. By a sacrifice of cargo space she could carry 285 more third-class passengers. A different arrangement of space would enable 1500 troops and 400 horses to be carried in addition to the other passengers. If entirely devoted to troops, the ship could convey 3000 men and 400 horses at once with the proper stores.

The Orient has been built, for the new line of Australian steam navigation, which is named after her, by Messrs. John Elder and Co., of Glasgow. The other vessels of this line are the Lusitania, the Cuzco, the Chimborazo, the Garonne, the Aconcagua, and the John Elder. One of these leaves London every four weeks, and one leaves Australia at the same time, for the return passage. They take in the mails at Plymouth, carrying them without subsidy, and touch at St. Vincent and the Cape on their voyage out. The Orient is expected to make the passage in less time than her sister ships have done, but the Chimborazo lately came from Adelaide to Plymouth in thirty-seven days ten hours, including delay in the Suez Canal and stoppages for coaling. Her engines are of 5400-horse power, and the average speed with which she ran the distance from Greenock to Margate was fourteen and a half knots, or more than fifteen miles, an hour. The ship is barque rigged, with four masts, has three iron decks, and is divided into thirteen water-tight compartments, by bulkheads, while, as a security against fire, from the lower to the main deck, she is divided into six compartments by five fire-proof bulkheads, fitted with fire-proof doors. She has been equipped beyond the requirements of her class, 100 A1, the highest at Lloyds', and has satisfied Government inspection as regards her defence by means of water-tight compartments and coal bunkers, so that she would be available if requisitioned in time of war as a cruiser or troopship. Her coal bunkers are so placed as to protect her engines, while they carry coal enough to keep her at sea, steaming full speed, for forty days, and she could not be sunk by penetration of less three of her water-tight compartments.

The engines, also made by Messrs. John Elder and Co., merit particular attention, having three cylinders instead of the common number of two ; one is high-pressure, with 60 in. diameter, the others low-pressure, 85 in. diameter. The crank-shaft is built in separate pieces, shrunk together and keyed, the diameter of the shaft being 20 in., and that of the crank-pins, which are of steel, 21 in. The propeller is four-bladed, the boss being of annealed cast-iron and the blade of cast-steel, specially made for the purpose by Messrs. Vickers, of Sheffield. The blades are bent backwards to diminish vibration. The diameter of the screw is 22 ft., and the pitch 30 ft. The condenser contains nearly 12,000 square feet of cooling surface, and the water for condensation is circulated by means of two independent combined steam centrifugal pumps, made by Messrs. Gwynne and Co., of London. The condensing surface and the capacity of the centrifugal pumps are made larger than they otherwise would be because the temperature of the water on part of the voyage home—namely, in the Red Sea—is so high that an unusually large quantity of it is required to cool and so condense the steam. The reversing engine is a special feature. Moving a lever not only stops the engines when at full speed, but immediately turns them full speed astern, and this motion has been so simplified that Lady Gertrude Boyle, on visiting the engine-room during the experimental cruise on the Clyde, easily stopped and reversed the engines when going at their maximum speed—that is to say, a young lady with one movement of her arm did what was tantamount to reining in 5600 horses. The boilers are four in number, 15 ft. 6 in. diameter, by 17 ft. 6 in. long. They contain twenty-four furnaces, each 4 ft. diameter by 6 ft. long, and the working pressure is 75 lb. on the square inch. The furnaces are constructed with special arrangements for the economical consumption of Australian coal on the passage home. From the results obtained it has been definitely proved that the consumption of coal will be economical at the speed at which it is intended she should run. The engines worked very smoothly without priming on the trip. The special arrangements of the machinery are due to the ingenuity of Mr. A. D. Bryce, the able superintendent of this department for John Elder and Co.

A great feature of the first-class accommodation is the splendid saloon forward, free from the engine-room, free from berths, running through from side to side, 44 feet square, and very lofty. It is fitted with electro-plated brass furniture, carpeted with a pattern by William Morris, and opening into the music saloon above, where, amid ferns and dracænas growing as plentifully as in the Sunbeam, a piano and an organ are to be placed. Here are elaborate wood carvings and ornamentation in patterns of the English Renaissance of the nineteenth century. The third-class accommodation supplies separate cabins with two berths for £18 per berth, and berths approached by separate passages for £15. The crew's forecastle is very spacious and comfortable. The chief saloon passengers have a promenade deck of 160 feet long, and the whole breadth of the vessel for their exclusive use, whilst the interior fittings of the dining-saloons, music-saloon, smoking-rooms, and passengers' cabins are of an elegant description.

The vessel is fitted with patent hand and steam steering gear, steam windlass, five powerful steam winches, two condensers for supplying fresh water, four large life-boats and five other boats; punkahs worked by steam in the chief dining-saloon, pneumatic bells to all saloon state-rooms, speaking-tubes and telegraphs. There are sixteen steam-engines, for different purposes, in the ship. The arrangements for a constant and ample supply of fresh water are such as might suffice for a town. The large tanks fitted below the orlop deck in the after-part of the ship hold about eighty tons. These are, of course, filled when the ship leaves the docks ; but to keep up the supply required for daily use there are two large condensers, which will condense, if required, 200 gallons per minute. The water when leaving the condenser enters a cooling tank fitted with a large spreader or aerator. From this tank it runs direct to the main tank, from which it is again pumped by a small steam-pump in the engine-room to a very large tank fitted on the promenade-deck, whence it runs to every compartment into smaller tanks. Ice-rooms are fitted on the lower deck for carrying sixty tons of ice. As a protection against fire, the sea can be admitted bodily into any two of the thirteen water-tight compartments without sinking the ship. The protection against drowning is supplied by four life-boats, carrying eighty each ; two cutters to convey ninety each, a gig and a mail-boat calculated to sustain forty-five each : a large steam-launch and twenty-six life-rafts, each capable of saving from forty to sixty people. In every berth in every class is a life-jacket which, rolled up, might be used as a bolster. Cattle enough to stock a farm are carried to provide fresh meat and milk on the voyage. A smaller ship of the line takes out six bullocks, one hundred sheep, 300 dozen of poultry, and embarks twelve bullocks more at the Cape. Mosses' and Mitchell's automatic ventilators, used in the British and American navies, are fitted to all the lower decks of the ship. When scuppers are closed in stormy weather, these ventilators increase in activity and expel the foul air through gigantic cowls. A special ventilator of Mr. Shepherd's (marine superintendent to the Orient Company) keeps the first and second class cabins sweet.

The steam-ship Orient was, by the liberality of the Orient Steam Navigation Company, thrown open to inspection, at moderate entrance charges, during three days of last week and on Monday last, for the benefit of five benevolent institutions—namely, the Dreadnought Seamen's Hospital, the East London Hospital for Children, the Poplar Hospital for Accidents, the Merchant Seamen's Orphan Asylum, and the Royal Alfred Merchant Seamen's Institution. The ship was thronged with visitors during the greater part of those days, and the sum of £872 was raised by this exhibition.

Article from the 'Illustrated London News' of 4th October 1879 describing the new steamship *Orient* (2), then the largest ship in the world after the *Great Eastern*.[Collection of the late Michael Jones]

Orient (2) in the 1880s with turtleback poop and topgallant-forecastle. *[Peter Newall collection]*

Four-masters of the 1880s

Orient (1) with her four tall masts and raked twin funnels set the style for the first generation of handsome Orient and P.S.N.C. Australian liners. Orient's first steel-hulled ship, the unfortunate *Austral* of 1881 which sank whilst coaling at Sydney, was followed by the even larger *Ormuz* (1) in 1886. *Ormuz* was also the first Orient ship with triple-expansion engines. For the first six years of the joint service P.S.N.C. used existing tonnage transferred from the South American run. In 1886 and 1887 its first purpose-built ships for the Australian line entered service, *Orizaba* and *Oroya*. Not only were these ships the first P.S.N.C. ocean-going ships with straight stems, they were also the first P.S.N.C. vessels to be constructed at Barrow-in-Furness. One of the reasons for the move away from the Clyde may have been the restructuring of the John Elder yard into the Fairfield Shipbuilding and Engineering Co. Ltd. *Orizaba* and *Oroya* were broadly similar to the Orient Line ships and, a few years later, they were joined by two new smaller versions, *Orotava* and *Oruba*, which had been designed for the Valparaiso service.

In April 1886 the port of Tilbury opened for business and, in January the following year, Orient Line started operations from these new London docks. By the end of the decade all the early P.S.N.C. ships had returned to the South American service whilst *Lusitania* and *Cuzco*, which had been given new triple-expansion engines, remained on the Australian run. In 1889 Orient Line became one of the pioneer cruise ship operators when *Chimborazo* and *Garonne* (1) were withdrawn for much of the year for 'special yachting cruises' to the Mediterranean and Norway. This first step into the cruise market was a great success and *Chimborazo, Garonne* (1) and *Lusitania* were used extensively for cruising in the 1890s.

The final break with sail

Ophir, the first Orient ship completed after the retirement of James Anderson, entered service in 1891, a year after Anderson, Anderson and Co. sold the last of its sailing ships. As if to herald a break with the past, the Napier-built *Ophir* only had two masts and no yards for auxiliary sail. She was the first ship on the Australia service with twin screws and

was designed to Admiralty requirements for conversion into an armed merchant cruiser. Her funnels were widely spaced because of the separation of her engine machinery to reduce shell damage in times of conflict. Although she was an expensive ship to operate because of her large coal consumption, *Ophir* is best remembered for her time as a royal yacht when she carried the future King George V and Queen Mary on a tour of the colonies in 1901.

The 1890s were tough times for Orient Line with a significant downturn in Australian trading and another serious accident whilst coaling, this time at Tilbury in 1896, when *Orotava* sank at her berth with the loss of four lives. After the problems with operating *Ophir* at a profit, Orient returned to Fairfield for the next two ships, *Omrah* of 1898 and *Orontes* (1) of 1902. *Omrah* was a revelation when she first appeared with her large 76-foot funnel and two short pole masts. Her magnificent two-deck high dining saloon with domed skylight could seat 108 first class passengers. She also had a much greater cargo capacity than any of the earlier ships with her reefer space able to hold 27,000 carcasses of frozen mutton. *Orontes* (1) was an enlarged version of *Omrah* but with a slightly shorter funnel and the first Orient ship with quadruple expansion engines.

Orient-Pacific Line and the arrival of Royal Mail

The final P.S.N.C. Australian ship was *Ortona*, which was completed in October 1899. By now the joint mail contract with P&O had been renewed, although with a reduction in the journey time between London and Melbourne to 31 days 6 hours. Many of the earlier ships had their funnels heightened around this time, possibly to improve draught to the furnaces and hence increase speed for the new mail contract. The financial problems for Orient which had continued for most of the 1890s improved and on 1st August 1900 the company was reconstructed. The Orient Steam Navigation Co. Ltd. was wound up and a new company, Orient Steam Navigation Co. Ltd., formed. The capital was sub-divided into preferred and deferred shares. Frederick Green and Co. and Anderson, Anderson and Co. held almost all the deferred shares (which later became ordinary shares) and continued as managers of the company. A new

Ormuz (1) (above top) and *Orizaba* as built (middle), both photographed off Gravesend by F.C. Gould. *Oruba's* profile (right) was spoilt by her funnels being too close together.

[National Maritime Museum G631, G502 and G2193].

agreement was also reached with P.S.N.C. which included changing the name of the joint service to the Orient-Pacific Line in 1901. The O.S.N.C. letters were also dropped from the flag and this became the Orient Line house flag until 1966. The mail contract was renewed in April 1905 with an annual subsidy of £120,000. It also stipulated that only white labour be employed on the ships.

On his birthday in 1903, the forty-year-old Owen Philipps (later Lord Kylsant) took over the helm as chairman of the Royal Mail Steam Packet Company. One of his first tasks was to obtain a supplemental charter to Royal Mail's archaic Royal Charter of 1839, which would allow the company to obtain shares in other companies. This resulted in the purchase on 26th February 1906 of P.S.N.C.'s half-share in Orient-Pacific Line and four of its ships - *Oroya*, *Orotava*, *Oruba* and *Ortona*. The whole of P.S.N.C. was acquired by Royal Mail in 1910.

The name of the joint service was altered to Orient-Royal Mail Line whilst the colours of the fleet were changed to those of the Royal Mail Steam Packet Co., i.e. buff funnel and vents with black hull and white superstructure. The management of the company, however, was retained by Anderson, Anderson and Co. and Frederick Green and Co. Owen Philipps was unhappy about the management agreement as he wanted greater control and a bigger share of the business. Things came to a head when Royal Mail tried unsuccessfully to negotiate direct with the Australian Government for a share of the Australian mail contract. After the contract was again awarded jointly to Orient and P&O, on

12th July 1907 Royal Mail gave eighteen months notice of its intent to withdraw from the joint service. In a final attempt to influence Australian opinion, Royal Mail sent one of its 'A' liners *Asturias* (12,015/1908) on her maiden voyage to Australia in January 1908. Although she was the largest ship to visit Australian ports at that time, at 16 knots she was too slow for the mail contract and only did one further round voyage in 1909 prior to the final Royal Mail sailing of *Ortona* from Tilbury on 30th April. The Royal Mail agreement with Orient Line officially ended on 15th May 1909.

Orient Steam Navigation Company Ltd. goes it alone
The 1908 mail contract was worth £170,000 per annum in subsidies and the managers of Orient were determined that they could maintain the fortnightly mail service independently. Unable to raise sufficient capital to finance the building of five 12,000gt ships, the largest ever seen in Australia, the managers gave personal guarantees to the shipbuilders for the initial money. Favourable repayment terms were also negotiated and the order was spread over a number of yards, with three built on the Clyde and two by Workman, Clark and Co. Ltd. in Belfast. The new vessels were delivered between May and November 1909. The first to arrive was *Orsova* (1) and with her twin funnels and Admiralty cowls she became the template for the next generation of Orient liners, which culminated in *Orontes* (2) of 1929. The new vessels also had five cargo holds and carried over 1,000 passengers.

Left: The fifth in Royal Mail's A-class series, *Asturias* at Sydney. In 1923 she became the cruise ship *Arcadian* and was scrapped in 1933. The building behind the ship's funnel is Hill, Clark and Co.'s wool store, which also features prominently in the view of *Harbinger* on page 46.
[Ian Farquhar collection]

Below: *Orsova* (1), the first of five new 12,000-ton liners delivered in 1909.
[J. and M. Clarkson collection]

Three further ships completed in 1909.

Above: *Otway* at Hobart during the fruit season.   [Ian Farquhar collection]

Right: *Osterley* photographed by William Livermore at Sydney.
          [Ian Farquhar collection]

Below: *Otranto* (1) in the Thames.
          [Peter Newall collection]

Right: *Orvieto* of 1909 photographed by Williamson Brothers at Hobart.
[Ian Farquhar collection]

Below: *Orama* (1) of 1911 as an armed merchant cruiser during the First World War photographed at Sydney by William Livermore.
[Ian Farquhar collection]

Orama (1), the final ship of the pre-war fleet was completed in 1911 as a replacement for *Ormuz* (1), the last of the four masters which, despite her age, was sold on to Compagnie de Navigation Sud Atlantique and was only scrapped in 1922. Although she looked similar to the earlier five ships, the slightly larger *Orama* (1) was unique. She was the sole Orient liner with triple screws and also the first to use a turbine, albeit in combination with two four-cylinder triple-expansion engines.

The First World War and the immediate post-war era
At the outbreak of war, Orient Line had a fleet of nine liners with construction underway on the new *Ormonde* which was just under 15,000gt and the first with a cruiser stern. Most of the ships were requisitioned as either armed merchant cruisers or troopships and by 1917 Orient Line had no ships on the Australian run. The war also went badly for Orient with the loss of four ships including *Omrah* and three of the new liners *Otway, Otranto* (1) and *Orama* (1). Three were

sunk by German submarines whilst *Otranto* (1) was wrecked after a collision with the P&O liner *Kashmir* which resulted in a great loss of life. Unlike other major British companies, Orient Line did not manage any captured German ships during the war. However, it managed five ex-German passenger ships for the Shipping Controller between 1919 and 1921 and a number of these ships operated to Australia.

Before the end of the war, the six partners in Frederick Green and Co. (three Devitts and three Greens) made it known that they wished to retire from the business. A deal was struck with P&O's chairman Lord Inchcape whereby the Frederick Green and Co. share of the Orient Line management contract would be handed over to the Inchcape-owned Gray, Dawes and Co. and a new management company formed in 1919 called Anderson, Green and Co. Ltd. The remaining half of the shares was held by members of the Anderson family who were directors of the new concern.

H·M·TROOPSHIP "FRIEDRICHSRUH"
FLYING ARMISTICE FLAG
EUROPEAN WAR.

Orient Line managed five ex-German passenger liners for the Shipping Controller between 1919 and 1921.

Above: The photo of *Friedrichsruh* at Sydney is unusual because it shows the Armistice flag on the stern. The same flag can be seen on *Rio Pardo* on page 124.
[Peter Newall collection)

Right: *Rio Pardo*
[Peter Newall collection]

Lower: *Huntsgreen* ex-*Derfflinger*.
[J. and M. Clarkson collection]

Lord Inchcape also recommended '...joining up with the Orient Company. We have lost fifteen of our mail steamers and we shall have the help of the Orient steamers until such time as we are able to rebuild', and on 11th December 1918 the P&O Board agreed to acquire a controlling 51% interest in Orient Steam Navigation Company Ltd. By 1921, the P&O shareholding increased to just over 54%. Despite the Inchcape and P&O involvement, however, Anderson, Green and Co. Ltd. remained effectively independent with the Anderson family still firmly in control. Anderson, Green also continued to be involved in the ship and insurance broking and chartering and forwarding agency business.

Towards the end of 1919, services to Australia started to get back to normal although Orient was desperately short of capacity with only five operational liners including *Ormonde*, which was eventually completed in 1917, and the 1902 *Orontes* (1), which was nearing the end of her career. Australasian United Steam Navigation's *Indarra* (9,735/1912) was chartered but she was dropped after only two voyages because she was too slow for the service. As a stopgap until the arrival of new replacements for the war losses, three former Norddeutscher Lloyd passenger ships were bought from the Shipping Controller in 1920 and 1921.

Above: *Ormonde* at Cape Town during the First World War.
[*Ship Society of South Africa/Martin Leendertz collection*]

Right: *Indarra* at Sydney in 1919. Note the funnels in Orient Line colours. Built in 1912 by William Denny and Bros., Dumbarton for the Australian United Steam Navigation Co. Ltd., Fremantle she was sold in 1920 and renamed *Pays de Waes*. In 1923 she became *Horai Maru* and as a hospital ship was torpedoed on 1st March 1942 at Bantam Bay, west Java. [*Peter Newall collection*]

Three former Norddeutscher Lloyd liners were bought from the Shipping Controller in 1920 and 1921 as a stopgap until the arrival of new replacements for war losses.

Above: *Omar* ex-*Königin Luise*
      [Peter Newall collection]

Right: *Orcades* (1) ex-*Prinz Ludwig*
      [Peter Newall collection]

Below: *Ormuz* (2) ex-*Zeppelin* photographed at Sydney.
      [Ian Farquhar collection]

A new fleet and innovative ships

Instead of joining the rush for replacement tonnage at war's end, Anderson, Green wisely waited until shipbuilding costs settled down in the early 1920s before placing orders for new ships. The contract for the first of five new 20,000gt liners, *Orama* (2), was awarded to the warship builders Vickers Ltd. of Barrow-in-Furness, which was desperate for work, and undercut its Clyde and Birkenhead rivals. From then on, with the exception of *Oronsay* (1) of 1925, all Orient passenger ships came from Barrow - a successful partnership which lasted until 1960 with the last Orient liner, *Oriana*.

The five turbine-driven ships completed between 1924 and 1929 were a continuation of the pre-war Orient Line series of vessels with two funnels bearing the distinctive Admiralty-type cowls. These liners were also designed to carry over 1,200 emigrants in relatively austere third class accommodation and almost 600 first class passengers in opulent surroundings with period decoration. The final ship in this group, *Orontes* (2), was slightly different in that she was given a raked bow. The introduction of the new ships also saw a change in the schedule of sailings to Australia. During the peak period of travel, October to March, fortnightly sailings were maintained whilst for the European summer, April to September, these were reduced to monthly departures. This allowed the ships to be used extensively for cruising in Northern Europe and the Mediterranean throughout the 1920s and 1930s.

The five 20,000-tonners of the 1920s.

Opposite upper: *Orama* (2) on trials.
[Ships in Focus collection]

Opposite lower: *Oronsay* (1) photographed at Sydney just prior to the Second World War by Dr. E.M. Humphery.
[Ian Farquhar collection]

This page upper: *Otranto* (2) in the Suez Canal. [Ambrose Greenway collection]

Right: *Orford.*
[J. and M. Clarkson collection]

This page below: *Orontes* (2).
[Ian Farquhar collection]

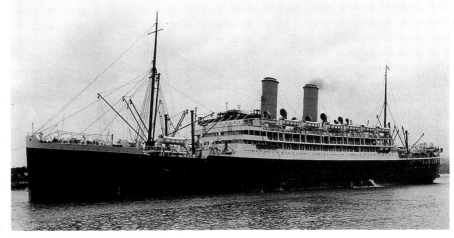

In the early 1930s Orient Line experienced changing conditions on the Australian route. Emigration was down because of the Depression and developing tastes meant that passengers who could not afford the first class fare were no longer satisfied with the stark conditions in third class. By the mid-1930s, the third class capacity on the 20,000 tonners was reduced and renamed tourist class. This was also a time of great innovation in design, and the company decided to build a ship which would be modern and comfortable for all passengers. Colin (later Sir Colin) Anderson was chosen to oversee the design of the new liner and a young New Zealand architect, Brian O'Rorke, who had never worked on a ship project before, was chosen to design all the passenger accommodation. The result of this collaboration was the 1935 Orion, one of the finest British liners of the twentieth century.

Whilst the style of Orion and her sister Orcades (2) of 1937 was undoubtedly Orient Line, the basic hull design of the two ships conformed to a P&O standard type which evolved from the turbo-electric liners Strathnaver and Strathaird of 1931 and 1932. The engine machinery and dimensions of the next three Straths, Strathmore (23,428/1935), Stratheden (23,722/1937) and Strathallan (23,722/1938) were broadly similar to those of the Orient pair. With the arrival of the Straths, P&O also introduced a new livery i.e. white hull and buff funnel in place of the dreary black hulls and funnels and stone superstructure. Orient did the same with Orion and Orcades (2) but with a much more imaginative colour scheme. The corn-coloured hull with green boot topping, which had been trialed on Orama (2) in 1934, was very effective and gave the new Orient ships a distinctive air which set them apart from other liners.

The 1920s-built two-funnelled ships were sent to Barrow in the mid-1930s for reductions in their passenger capacity. Here is *Orford* passing *Orion* and P&O's semi-completed *Strathmore,* which shared *Orion's* hull shape, engine machinery and dimensions. *[Sankeys Ltd.]*

Although *Strathmore's* hull was similar to *Orion,* she was fitted with a traditional fore and main mast arrangement.
[J. and M. Clarkson collection]

The new hull colour for *Orion* was a warm corn colour with green boot topping and this had been trialed on *Orama* (2) during a voyage to Australia in October 1934. As well as being an attractive feature, this colour was less likely to fade and reduced the hull temperature by a few degrees, a welcome relief in the stifling heat of the Red Sea.

Above: *Orion* photographed by Allan C. Green at Melbourne. *[Ian Farquhar collection.]*

Below: *Orama* (2) off Tilbury in her new colours. *[R.A.F. Museum/Charles E. Brown collection 5445-8]*

Evolved from *Orion*, *Orcades* (2) had the same style interiors with large uninterrupted spaces, simple furniture, beautifully woven carpets and stylish upholstery. The design of the main first class lounge (below) would not seem out of place today and it is a pity that few of the furnishings on these two ships appear to have survived. *[Upper: Ballast Trust, lower: Peter Newall collection]*

War losses and more new ships

The Second World War was almost a repeat of the 1914-18 conflict for Orient Line. Half the fleet was lost by enemy action and it was some time after the war that normal operations resumed to Australia. The war losses included *Orford*, *Orama* (2), *Oronsay* (1) and *Orcades* (2), the last two being sunk by submarine attack a day apart. To add insult to injury, the head office was hit during an air raid in 1941 and many of the company records destroyed.

The war-managed ships included two Liberties, the first cargo-only vessels operated by Orient Line, and four Dutch liners from Stoomvaart Maatschappij 'Nederland' which were run by Orient but with Dutch crew. From 1945 to 1958 the company also managed the former Deutsche Ost-

Afrika-Linie flagship *Pretoria*, which had been converted into the troopship *Empire Doon*, later renamed *Empire Orwell*.

In July 1948, a new Companies Act came into force, which required Orient Steam Navigation Co. Ltd. to adopt new Articles of Association. As a result, the control of Orient Steam Navigation Co. Ltd. was vested in a board of directors whilst Anderson, Green and Co. Ltd. had its own board, not all of whom were directors of Orient. Prior to this, all directorial functions were undertaken by the management company. At the same time, the remaining shares in Anderson, Green and Co. Ltd. were purchased by Orient and the company became a wholly-owned subsidiary, although retaining the management of Orient Line.

Two of the war-managed Dutch ships: *Christiaan Huygens* (above) and *Johan de Witt* (below). *[Both: L.L.von Munching collection]*

31

Right: *Empire Orwell* passing through the Suez Canal in 1955.
[Ambrose Greenway collection]

Below: *Orcades* (3) leaving Singapore in 1960.
[Ambrose Greenway collection]

Orion took the first post-war departure for Australia on 25th February 1947. She was joined later that year by *Ormonde* which had been converted into a full-time emigrant ship and in 1948 and 1949 by the remaining survivors *Orontes* (2) and *Otranto* (2). Between 1948 and 1954 Orient Line also took delivery of three 28,000gt liners built to replace ships lost in the war. The first of these was *Orcades* (3) in 1948. Not only was she the largest and fastest ship on the Australian run to that date, but she also had a striking profile which showed again the forward-thinking ethos of Orient Line and its management. She was followed nine months later by P&O's *Himalaya* (27,955/1949), which was also built at Barrow using the same hull form. Whilst *Himalaya* was a traditional-looking ship with foremast and a large single funnel, *Orcades* (3) had no tall masts, whilst her bridge and signal mast were set back and almost merged with the funnel. Despite a serious fire whilst fitting out, the second in the trio, *Oronsay* (2), arrived in 1951 and was similar to *Orcades* (3) except that she had a large signal mast in place of the tripod mast. The final ship, *Orsova* (2) was the first large all-welded liner and the first to dispense with masts except for kingposts. Because of soot problems on her sisters, she was fitted with a 'Welsh Hat' on the funnel and this feature also appeared on the earlier pair. As they had done before the war with *Orion* and *Orcades* (2), Sir Colin Anderson and Brian O'Rorke again teamed up to oversee the interior design of the new trio.

Final integration with P&O

Following the withdrawal the previous year of Canadian-Australasian Line's *Aorangi* (17,491/1924), on 1st January 1954 *Oronsay* opened up an experimental new route from Sydney via Auckland across the Pacific to San Francisco and Vancouver. This continued for occasional voyages and in February 1958 it became a joint service with P&O known as Orient and Pacific Lines. This integration led to the eventual loss of Orient Line's independence and, on 10th February 1960, P&O made a successful offer to purchase the remaining 46% of the Orient Steam Navigation Company Ltd. ordinary shares it did not already own. On 1st May 1960 two new P&O subsidiaries were formed: P&O-Orient Lines Passenger Services Ltd., which looked after the operation of the P&O and Orient Line passenger ships, whilst the management of the ships was undertaken by P&O-Orient Management Ltd. Although the vessels sailed under their own livery and house flags, they were advertised as P&O-Orient Lines instead of Orient and Pacific Lines. In 1964 a new livery was introduced for all ships in the P&O-Orient Lines fleet: white hull (from P&O); green boot-topping (from Orient Line) and yellow funnels. Despite this change, the separate house flags continued to be flown.

Above: *Oronsay* (2) in the Great Bitter Lake, Suez Canal. *[Ambrose Greenway collection]*

Below: *Orsova* (2) on trials. *[Ambrose Greenway collection]*

Oriana on trials during which she attained a mean speed of 30.64 knots over the Arran Measured Mile. Weather conditions at the time were poor with a Force 7 wind. *[Peter Newall collection]*

Garonne (2) on trials. *[Ambrose Greenway collection]*

Anderson, Green meanwhile took on a new lease of life as shipbrokers. On 27th January 1975, Anderson, Green and Co. Ltd. merged with another P&O-owned broker which had a long association with the Australian trade, Birt, Potter and Hughes Ltd. The new concern, Anderson, Hughes and Co. Ltd. is still in business within the P&O group and reports its results through P&O Australia where it has a bigger presence than in the UK.

In November 1960, Orient took delivery of its final passenger liner, the revolutionary *Oriana* which was unlike any passenger liner built before. Much has been written about her controversial design with two small funnels (the aft one was a dummy) and rather boxy superstructure which was not to everyone's taste. Again the contrast between her and P&O's conventional-looking *Canberra* (45,733/1961) speaks volumes about the differences between the two companies. There is also a sense of irony in the fact that *Oriana* still exists, albeit as a visitor attraction in Dalian, China, whilst *Canberra* was broken up in Pakistan in 1997. On her trials, *Oriana* managed over 30 knots and sailed for Australia on her maiden voyage on 3rd December 1960. When she reached Sydney 27 days later she became yet another Orient liner which was the largest and fastest on the Australian run. Although registered at London, her homeport was Southampton, instead of Orient's traditional home, Tilbury.

Mention should also be made of Orient Line's first and only tanker which was ordered as part of P&O's initially misguided Group tanker programme which allocated ships to individual companies, including Orient, P&O, New Zealand Shipping Co., British India, Moss Hutchison, and Strick Line, none of whom had any tanker experience. *Garonne* (2) was built at Vickers-Armstrongs' Newcastle-upon-Tyne yard in 1959 and had a relatively small funnel. Her first voyage was a British Petroleum charter to the Persian Gulf. In 1963 she was absorbed into P&O's tanker subsidiary, Trident Tankers Ltd., set up in 1962.

In 1965, the P&O take-over was complete with the purchase of the outstanding Orient preference shares and on 30th September 1966 the Orient Line flag came down for the last time. This is not the end of the story, however, as the Orient Steam Navigation Co. Ltd. name was revived, for registration purposes, for a series of liquid gas carriers and OBO (ore/bulk/oil) vessels in P&O's Bulk Shipping Division from 1977 to 1987. The company was formally wound up on 3rd November 1998.

The Anderson connection also remained strong with Sir Donald Anderson Chairman of P&O from 1960 until his retirement in 1971, 130 years after James Anderson became a partner in James Thomson and Company, the trading company which grew into one of the most famous of all British liner companies.

The liquified gas carrier *Garmula*.
[G.R. Scott collection]

The ore/bulk/oil carrier *Jedforest*.
[G.R. Scott collection]

In 1964 the final quartet of Orient liners were painted in the new P&O-Orient Lines' corporate livery: white hull; green boot-topping and yellow funnels. Although they remained handsome-looking ships, the loss of the corn-coloured hull certainly made them less distinctive and unique.

Orcades (3) photographed in August 1967 at Cape Town. *[Robert Pabst]*

Oronsay (2) at Aden, 16th March 1966. *[Ambrose Greenway]*

Orsova (2) passing under the Sydney Harbour Bridge in 1965. *[Ambrose Greenway]*

Oriana leaving Woolloomooloo, Sydney in 1965. *[Ambrose Greenway]*

SHIPS OF ANDERSON, THOMSON AND CO. AND ANDERSON, ANDERSON AND CO.

The fleet list is complete from 1st January 1863, when James Anderson became a partner in Anderson, Thomson and Co. The partnership became Anderson, Anderson and Co. in December 1869.

AGNES 1863-1867 Wooden barque. West Indies trade.
O.N. 4271 339g 94.9 x 23.5 x 17.7 feet.
19.9.1842: Completed by Hilhouse, Hill and Co., Bristol.
29.9.1842: Registered at London in the ownership of James Thomson and Co., London as AGNES.
1867: Condemned.

POINT 1863-1879 Wooden barque. West Indies trade.
O.N. 10767 366g 105.3 x 23.0 x 17.8 feet.
1848: Completed by Fletcher, Son and Fearnall, Union Dock, Poplar.
12.9.1848: Registered at London in the ownership of James Thomson and Co., London as POINT.
15.9.1879: Sold to J. Bond and Son, London.
1880: Broken up.
1.11.1880: Register closed.

TRAVANCORE 1863-1865 Wooden barque. Australian trade.
O.N. 23315 582g 118.3 x 26.4 x 20.1 feet.
10.3.1848: Completed at Cochin for Duncan Campbell and partner, Cochin as TRAVANCORE.
10.4.1849: Sold to James Thomson and Co., London.
6.7.1849: Registered at London.
1865: Sold to James Shearer, Ardrossan.
8.11.1865: Registered at Glasgow.
1868: Registered owner Kenneth and Co., Glasgow.
1885: Sold to W. Goldfinch, Glasgow and demolished.
3.6.1885: Register closed.

CHEBUCTO 1863-1868 Wooden ship. West Indies trade.
O.N. 10557 409g 128.9 x 24.2 x 17.8 feet.
1851: Completed by Thomas Bilbe and Co., Rotherhithe.
26.6.1851: Registered at London in the ownership of James Thomson and Co., London as CHEBUCTO.
1859: Reduced to barque rig.
25.12.1868: Wrecked at Annotto Bay, Jamaica in a northerly gale.
12.2.1869: Register closed.

PRINCE RUPERT 1863-1864 Wooden barque. West Indies trade.
O.N. 26420 347g 100.0 x 23.0 x 17.8 feet.
20.3.1841: Completed by Green, Wigram and Green, Blackwall (Yard No. 250).
11.5.1841: Registered at London in the ownership of the Hudson Bay Company, London as PRINCE RUPERT.
9.12.1853: Sold to James Thomson and Co., London.
1864: Sold to William Redman and Co., Newcastle-upon-Tyne.
11.11.1864: Registered at Newcastle-upon-Tyne.
1867: Sold to William Cass, Goole.
10.10.1867: Registered at Goole.
14.11.1870: Foundered 25 miles north west of Le Mole St. Nicholas, Haiti.
26.1.1871: Register closed.

ORIENT (1) 1863-1879 Wooden ship. Australian trade.
O.N. 12981 1,033g 184.4 x 31.7 x 21.1 feet.
14.12.1853: Completed by Thomas Bilbe and Co., Rotherhithe.
18.1.1854: Registered at London in the ownership of James Thomson and Co., London as ORIENT.
1854: Chartered by British Government for trooping during the Crimean War as Transport No. 78.
10.1855: Became a hospital ship.
5.7.1856: First voyage Plymouth to Australia.
2.1.1862: Caught fire during a voyage from Cape Town to London. The passengers were transferred to another ship and the damaged cargo was discharged at Ascension Island.

Orient (1) passing Gibraltar in 1854 as a Crimean War transport. *[P&O Archives]*

Orient (1) in service as a coal hulk at Gibraltar. [National Maritime Museum P5179]

15.4.1879: Sold to Cox Brothers, Waterford.
18.12.1879: Registered at Waterford. Ran in the North American lumber trade.
1886: Reduced to barque rig, 960g.
1890: Sold to Smith, Imossi and Co., Gibraltar (agents for P&O) and became a coal hulk at Gibraltar.
13.3.1891: Register closed.
1925: Broken up at Gibraltar.

EVELINE 1863-1864 Wooden ship. West Indies trade.
O.N. 15488 808g 165.8 x 34.1 x 20.9 feet.
1853: Launched by E. Atkinson, Quebec for Hammond, London as EVELINE. Registered at London.
c 1855: Acquired by Anderson, Thomson and Co., London.
1864: Sold to R. Johnston, Aberdeen.
1866: Sold to William Lindsay and Co., Greenock
22.10.1881: Foundered in position 48.10 north by 38.40 west whilst on a voyage from Quebec to London with cargo of timber and deals. One life was lost.

CASSANGE 1863-1864 Wooden barque. West Indies trade.
O.N. 4605 348g 126.5 x 25.8 x 17.3 feet.
28.6.1854: Launched by William Pile Junior, North Shore, Monkwearmouth.
10.7.1854: Completed for Leadbitter, Sunderland as CASSANGE. Registered at Sunderland.
1857: Sold James Thomson and Co., London.
9.2.1857: Registered at London.
10.2.1864: Caught fire at sea.
13.4.1864: Register closed.

VERE 1863-1879 Wooden barque. West Indies trade.
O.N. 20399 396g 129.8 x 27.2 x 17.2 feet.
14.9.1857: Completed by W. Watson, Hylton, Sunderland.
29.10.1857: Registered at London in the ownership of James Thomson and Co., London as VERE.
31.5.1879: Sold to Edwin Smith, Plymouth.
27.5.1880: Registered at Plymouth.
29.4.1882: Register closed on sale to J.V. Hellberg, Sundsvall, Sweden.
1890: Owner registered as E.A. Enhörning.

1895: Registered at Kubikenborg, Sweden.
1896: Sold to G.P. Gudmundsson, Höganäs, Sweden.
1899: Broken up.

VENILIA 1863-1863 Wooden ship.
O.N. 12983 647g 147.6 x 29.4 x 19.7 feet.
24.8.1854: Completed at Sunderland for Shield as VENILIA. Registered at Newcastle-upon-Tyne.
1858: Sold to James Thomson and Co., London.
29.4.1858: Registered at London.
11.1863: Sold to John Baker, London
10.8.1869: Left Annotto Bay, Jamaica for London with general cargo and went missing with all 19 on board.
23.2.1870: Register closed.

WESTMORELAND 1863-1871 Wooden barque. West Indies trade.
O.N. 22182 452g 136.2 x 28.1 x 17.7 feet.
7.9.1858: Completed at North Hylton, Sunderland.
10.9.1858: Registered at London in the ownership of James Thomson and Co., London as WESTMORELAND.
14.7.1871: Wrecked at Bolt Head, 1.5 miles west of Salcombe, whilst on a voyage from Jamaica to London with general cargo

SOMASS 1863-1866 Wooden ship and later barque.
O.N. 13663 521g 136.6 x 24.5 x 16.0 feet.
1852: Completed by William Johnston, Chatham, New Brunswick.
24.12.1852: Registered at London in the ownership of Fry and Co., London as GOMELZA. London to Vancouver trade.
1860: After being 'wrecked', sold at Vancouver Island to James Thomson and Co., London and renamed SOMASS.
16.4.1866: Register closed.

CLARENDON 1863-1870 Wooden barque. West Indies trade.
O.N. 29016 468g 135.2 x 28.1 x 18.0 feet.
1860: Completed by Gowan, Berwick-upon-Tweed.
27.10.1860: Registered at London in the ownership of James Thomson and Co., London as CLARENDON.
23.12.1870: Blown ashore during a gale on a reef near Rendevous Point on west side of Turneffe Island, British Honduras whilst loading a cargo of mahogany.

The Murray. [State Library of South Australia]

Coonatto. [State Library of South Australia]

Yatala. [State Library of South Australia]

THE MURRAY 1863-1879 Wooden ship. Australian trade.
O.N. 29788 811g 193.0 x 33.2 x 20.2 feet.
25.5.1861: Completed by Alexander Hall and Co., Aberdeen (Yard No. 222).
3.7.1861: Registered at London in the ownership of James Thomson and Co., London as THE MURRAY.
20.10.1879: Registered at Aberdeen.
2.4.1880: Register closed on sale to O.L. Roed, Tønsberg, Norway and renamed FREIA.
10.12.1884: Lost at Koster on the eastern side of the outer Oslofjord whilst on a voyage from North Shields to Vrengen near Tønsberg with cargo of coal. The entire crew was lost.

CLAUDIA 1863-1871 Wooden barque. West Indies trade.
O.N. 24618 398g 103.0 x 26.5 x 18.5 feet.
4.4.1844: Completed by Austin and Mills, Southwick, Sunderland.
3.5.1844: Registered at London in the ownership of Joseph Colling and Co., London as CLAUDIA.
10.1862: Sold James Thomson and Co., London.
5.12.1871: Wrecked on the bar of the River Ulua, Honduras.
2.5.1872: Register closed.

COONATTO 1863-1876 Composite ship. Australian trade.
O.N. 47320 633g 160.2 x 29 x 18.7 feet.
1863: Completed by Thomas Bilbe and Co., Rotherhithe.
20.4.1863: Registered at London in the ownership of Anderson, Thomson and Co., London as COONATTO.
21.2 1876: Wrecked at Cuckmere Haven, just west of Flagstaff Point, Sussex, whilst on a voyage from Adelaide to London with cargo of wool and copper.
20.7.1876: Register closed.

RIO GRANDE 1863-1874 Wooden brigantine. West Indies trade.
O.N. 46620 267g 113.0 x 26.8 x 12.5 feet.
8.8.1863: Completed by John Harley, Beaubair's Island, New Brunswick for unknown owners as RIO GRANDE.
Registered at Miramichi and sold in London to Anderson, Thomson and Co. London.
16.11.1863: Registered at London.
3.6.1874: Wrecked at Antigua.
3.7.1874: Register closed.

CREDENDA 1864 CORNWALL 1867-1873 Wooden barque.
O.N. 20399/46625 443g 136.0 x 30.7 x 12.9 feet.
30.9.1863: Completed by O'Brien, Bathurst, New Brunswick for J. O'Brien, Miramichi as CREDENDA.
26.4.1864: Registered at London in the ownership of Anderson, Thomson and Co. London.
25.8.1864: Register closed on sale to foreigners, probably French.

1867: Given new keel and repaired. Re-acquired by Anderson, Thomson and Co. London.
17.12.1867: Re-registered at London with new O.N. 46625 and renamed CORNWALL
10.1869: Took first sailing on London to Valparaiso and Callao service.
30.11.1873: Wrecked on Florida Reef.
1.4.1874: Register closed.

THE GOOLWA 1864-1877 Composite ship. Australian trade.
O.N. 48750 718g 178.5 x 30.6 x 18.8 feet.
3.1864: Launched by Alexander Hall and Co., Aberdeen (Yard No. 237) as GOOLWA.
1.4.1864: Completed for Anderson, Thomson and Co., London.
29.4.1864: Registered at London as THE GOOLWA probably because another London-registered GOOLWA (O.N. 48675) had been completed the previous January.
1877: Sold to A. Lawrence, London.
1887: Sold to G. Cowper, Glasgow.
5.1.1888: Foundered about 100 miles south west of the Scillies whilst on a voyage from Glasgow and Cardiff to San Francisco with cargo of pig iron and coke.
9.3.1888: Register closed.

YATALA 1865-1872 Composite ship. Australian trade.
O.N. 52737 1,127g 203.4 x 34.6 x 21.1 feet.
1865: Completed by Thomas Bilbe and Co., Rotherhithe.
13.7.1865: Registered at London in the ownership of Anderson, Thomson and Co., London as YATALA.
28.3.1872: Wrecked at Audresselles, Gris Nez, north of Boulogne, whilst on a voyage from Adelaide to London with a cargo of wool.
10.5.1872: Register closed.

EDEN 1866-1881 Wooden barque. West Indies trade.
O.N. 56729 500g 139.0 x 28.8 x 17.6 feet.
27.4.1866: Completed by William Baldwin, Quebec for J. and H. Watson, Glasgow as TAMARAC.

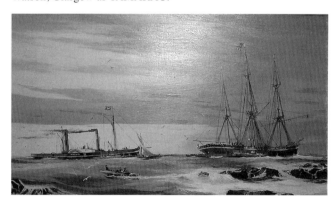

Above: Wreck of *Coonatto* at Cuckmere Haven in February 1876. Painting commissioned by The Salvage Association showing William Watkin's salvage tug *Anglia* (274/1866).
[Peter French collection]

Left: *The Goolwa*, probably photographed at Aberdeen in 1864.
[J. and M. Clarkson collection]

Darra rigged as a barque. *[Canterbury Museum, Christchurch, NZ. 2856 1/4]*

For fifty years *Darra* was a coal hulk at Lyttelton. Note the piles of coal on the quay behind her and the coal loader at the end of the wharf.   *[Wilkinson collection/Alexander Turnbull Library, Wellington F-11156-1/4]*

Darra at Lyttelton rigged as *Charlotte Jane,* one of the "first four ships" for the Canterbury centenary celebrations 1950.
[Canterbury Museum, Christchurch, NZ.3048 1/4]

In 1951 *Darra* was dismantled in dry dock at Lyttelton prior to being run ashore on Quail Island, Lyttelton.
[Wilkinson collection/Alexander Turnbull Library, Wellington NZ, F-11155-1/4]

1866: Acquired by Anderson, Anderson and Co., London and renamed EDEN.
19.11.1866: Registered at London.
11.2.1880: Registered at Aberdeen.
30.4.1881: Register closed on sale to G. Synnestvedt, Kragerø, Norway.
1884: Renamed UNION.
12.3.1890: Stranded on Horn Island, Rio Parana.
8.1890: Condemned.

DARRA 1867-1884 Composite ship. Australian trade.
O.N. 52729 999g 190.0 x 33.7 x 21.4 feet.
20.6.1865: Completed by Alexander Hall and Co., Aberdeen (Yard No. 241).
3.7.1865: Registered at London in the ownership of William Young, London as DARRA.
1867: Acquired by Anderson, Thomson and Co., London.
1879: Reduced to barque rig.
9.7.1880: Registered at Aberdeen.
11.10.1884: Sold to Trinder, Anderson and Co., London.
15.6.1888: Sold to the Australian Mercantile Loan and Guarantee Co. Ltd., Sydney.
1890: Sold to Thomas Cowlishaw, Sydney.
1892: Sold to James C. Ellis, Sydney.
1899: Gutted by fire at Sydney and sold to the Westport Coal Co. Ltd., Dunedin for use as a coal hulk at Lyttelton.
16.12.1950: Re-rigged as CHARLOTTE JANE one of the 'first four ships' for the Canterbury centenary. The 663g CHARLOTTE JANE (1848-1862) was owned by James Thomson and Co.
1951: Dismantled in dry-dock at Lyttelton and run ashore on Quail Island, Lyttelton just behind BELLEISLE. Despite an attempt by the New Zealand Army to blow her up in April 1953, her remains are still visible.

HANOVER 1867-1872 Wooden barque. West Indies trade.
O.N. 56766 299g 131.0 x 24.8 x 12.7 feet.
5.2.1867: Completed by Thomas Bilbe and Co., Rotherhithe.
25.2.67: Registered at London in the ownership of Anderson, Thomson and Co., London as HANOVER.
31.12.1872: Sold to William Robertson, London.
15.5.1874: Sailed from Newcastle, New South Wales for Tientsin with twelve crew and a cargo of coal and went missing.
14.1.1875: Registered closed.

CAMBRIAN 1868-1872 Wooden barque. West Indies trade.
O.N. 880 219g 91.6 x 21.4 x 14.9 feet.
19.12.1851: Completed by Robert White, Cowes.
16.12.1851: Registered at London in the ownership of Edward Jones and Co., London as CAMBRIAN.
1868: Acquired by Anderson, Thomson and Co., London.
13.10.1872: Wrecked at Grand Cayman.

TROPIC 1868-1881 Wooden barque. West Indies trade.
O.N. 60868 509g 141.0 x 29.5 x 17.9 feet.
20.6.1868: Completed by William Baldwin, Quebec for J. Bickell, Quebec as BEVERLY.
1868: Acquired by Anderson, Thomson and Co., London and renamed TROPIC.
30.9.1868: Registered at London.
21.10.1879: Registered at Aberdeen.
13.9.1881: Sold to T.T. Morrow, Liverpool.
12.4.1882: Foundered about 225 miles east of Uruguay in position 35.56 south by 49.26 west whilst on a voyage from Liverpool to Victoria, British Columbia with general cargo.
26.5.1882: Registered closed.

MAROON (1) 1868-1882 Wooden barque. West Indies trade.
O.N. 6947 362g 124.2 x 25 x 16.0 feet.
1.12.1855: Completed by Symons and Co., Bristol for their own account as JANE SYMONS.
1855: Registered at Bristol.
1868: Sold 'foreign' but acquired by Anderson, Thomson and Co., London and renamed MAROON.

24.11.1868: Registered at London.
1879: Registered at Aberdeen.
31.1.1882: Sold to James Cummins, Melbourne.
3.2.1882: Registered at Melbourne.
1889: Sold to Benjamin Jenkins, Sydney. Registered at Sydney.
24.5.1892: Registered at Hong Kong.
28.9.1892: Wrecked near on Craigie Island, Korea whilst on a voyage from Chefoo to Olga Bay in ballast with eight passengers

BELLEISLE 1868-1881 Wooden barque. West Indies trade.
O.N. 18585 380g 132.2 x 25.2 x 16.4 feet.
7.7.1857: Completed by Symons and Co., Bristol for their own account as PETER SYMONS.
9.7.1857: Registered at Bristol.
1868: Sold 'foreign' but acquired by Anderson, Thomson and Co., London and renamed BELLEISLE.
20.11.1868: Registered at London.
20.10.1879: Registered at Aberdeen.
12.10.1881: Sold to T. Brock, Glasgow.
1884: Sold to James C. Ellis, Sydney and registered at Sydney.
1893: Sold to the Union Steam Ship Co. of New Zealand Ltd., Dunedin.
8.1893: Registered at Dunedin. Used as coal hulk at Lyttelton, New Zealand.
28.10.1913: Registered closed.
1923: Demolished at Lyttelton and beached on Quail Island, Lyttelton Harbour. Sections of her hull are still visible at low tide.

GLENBROOK 1868-1877 Wooden brig. West Indies trade.
O.N. 45050 234g 99.0 x 25.7 x 14.7 feet.
9.1862: Launched by Gray, Sunderland.
2.10.1862: Completed for John Borradaile, London as GLENBROOK.
6.10.1862: Registered at London.
12.11.1868: Acquired by Anderson, Thomson and Co., London.
14.11.1877: Wrecked in Crooked Island Passage, Bahamas in position 23.02 north by 74.4 west whilst on a voyage from Jamaica to London with sugar and rum.
27.2.1878: Registered closed.

KIRKHAM 1869-1879 Iron ship. Australian/world-wide trade.
O.N. 17846 1,128g 201.9 x 34.2 x 21.7 feet.
15.11.1856: Launched by Laird Brothers, Birkenhead (Yard No. 195).
17.1.1857: Registered at Liverpool in the ownership of W.T. Jacob and Co., Liverpool as KIRKHAM.
1869: Acquired by Anderson, Thomson and Co., London.
12.10.1869: Registered at London.
20.10.1879: Registered at Aberdeen.
1880: Sold to M.G. Amsinck, Hamburg, Germany and renamed CERES. Reduced to barque rig.
28.8.1888: Wrecked on the Pajaros Islands, Chile whilst on a voyage from Hamburg to Carrizal Bay, Chile with cargo of coal.

ROMULUS 1872-1881 Wooden barque. Australian/world-wide trade.
O.N. 27325 724g 153.9 x 32.3 x 19.6 feet.
1859: Completed by William Olive, St. John, New Brunswick as ROMULUS.
1.6.1859: Registered at Bristol in the ownership of John Buckle, Bristol.
1872: Acquired by Anderson, Anderson and Co., London.
6.2.1872: Registered at London.
21.10.1879: Registered at Aberdeen.
1880: Sold to Richard Jolly, London.
23.4.1880: Registered at London.
8.7.1880: Register closed on sale to H. Ericksen, Porsgrund, Norway.
1886: Registered owner became Sophus Erichsen, Porsgrund.
15.10.1893: Abandoned in North Atlantic whilst on a voyage from Pensacola to Antwerp with cargo of pitch pine.

ATLANTIC 1871-1874 Wooden barque. Australian/world-wide trade.

O.N. 39042 628g 148.1 x 32.2 x 19.8 feet.
1855: Completed by Yeo, Prince Edward Island for Carmichael as ATLANTIC. Registered at Prince Edward Island.
1860: Sold to W. Yeo.
1871: Acquired by Anderson, Anderson and Co., London.
15.6.1871: Registered at London.
13.12.1874: Abandoned.
1.1875: Wreck cast ashore at St. Nazaire.
6.3.1875: Register closed.

HEATHER BELL 1871-1881 Wooden barque. Australian/world-wide trade.

O.N. 32005 490g 153.9 x 28.3 x 17.8 feet.
1855: Completed by John Duthie, Aberdeen for Thomas Brown and Co, London as HEATHER BELL. Registered at Hobart Town, Tasmania.
5.1861: Sold to Samuel Tulloch, Launceston, Tasmania.
24.2.1871: Acquired by Anderson, Anderson and Co., London.
9.4.1872: Registered at London.
17.10.1879: Registered at Aberdeen.
15.9.1881: Sold to Edward Miles, Melbourne.
30.9.1881: Registered at Melbourne.
1882: Sold to George Bailey, Adelaide. Registered at Adelaide.
1889: Sold to Herbert Cuthbertson, Newcastle, New South Wales.
10.1892: Condemned
1894: Broken up at Balmain, Sydney.

Heather Bell. [State Library of South Australia]

PUDSEY DAWSON 1871-1874 Wooden ship.

O.N. 12938 737g 149.2 x 31.5 x 21.0 feet.
11.11.1852: Launched by L. Kennedy and Co., Whitehaven.
25.1.1853: Registered at Liverpool in the ownership of Henry Hoskins and Robert Hutchison, Liverpool as PUDSEY DAWSON.
1856: Sold to Benjamin Nicholson and Co., Liverpool.
21.1.1871: Acquired by Anderson, Anderson and Co., London.
1874: Sold to Moore and Rawle, Plymouth.
12.1.1874: Registered at Plymouth.
1885: Sold to C.J. King and Son, Plymouth.
1888: Became a hulk.
6.12.1888: Register closed.

COSMOPOLITE 1872-1876 Wooden ship.

O.N. 68390 786g 160.0 x 37 x 19.3 feet.
29.11.1854: Launched by Cornelis Gips and Zonen, Dordrecht.
1.1855: Delivered to Gebr. Blussé, Dordrecht as KOSMOPOLIET. A famous Dutch clipper, she was the first of three with this name, the second and third being completed in 1865 and 1871.
1872: Acquired by Anderson, Anderson and Co., London and renamed COSMOPOLITE.
21.2.1873: Registered at London.
7.1876: Sold for use as a hulk.
26.10.1876: Register closed.

Dutch clipper Kosmopoliet. [K. Suyk collection]

JAMES DUNCAN 1872-1876 Wooden barque. West Indies trade.

O.N. 22022 345g 115.0 x 27.7 x 16.6 feet.
1859: Completed by James Hardie, Sunderland.
5.3.1859: Registered at Leith in the ownership of James Duncan, Leith as JAMES DUNCAN.
1872: Acquired by Anderson, Anderson and Co., London.
24.10.1872: Registered at London.
15.10.1876: Sold to Thomas Pattrick and Co., Wisbech.
6.7.1877: Registered at Wisbech.
1884: Sold to R. Williamson, Grangemouth.
31.3.84: Registered at Grangemouth.
24.5.1886: Register closed on sale to P. Wilhelmsen A/S, Copenhagen, Denmark. Reduced to schooner rig.
1896: Condemned.

HESPERUS 1873-1890 Iron ship. Australian trade.

O.N. 68500 1,859g 262.2 x 39.7 x 23.5 feet.
20.11.1873: Launched by Robert Steele and Co., Greenock (Yard No. 82).
23.12.1873: Registered at London in the ownership of Anderson, Anderson and Co., London as HESPERUS.
30.7.1880: Registered at Aberdeen
20.5.1890: Sold to Devitt and Moore, London for use as a cadet ship.
25.7.1899: Register closed on sale to Russian Government as a sail training ship. Owners registered as Trustees of Odessa Commercial School, Odessa and renamed GRAND DUCHESS MARIA NIKOLAEVNA.
1914: Refitted at Swan, Hunter and Wigham Richardson Ltd., Wallsend-on-Tyne. Later moved to Frederikshavn, Denmark and laid up for duration of the war.
1918: Taken over by Russian Volunteer Fleet and refitted at Newcastle.
11.1920: Laid up at Liverpool.
1921: Sold to the London and Foreign Trading Corporation Ltd., London (later became the London Steamship and Trading Corporation) and renamed SILVANA.
18.4.1921: Registered at London.
1923: Sold at Bordeaux by French courts to French citizens. Broken up at Genoa.
14.3.1923: Register closed.

VERONICA 1874-1884 Wooden barque. West Indies trade.

O.N. 28192 333g 127.5 x 25.3 x 17.2 feet.
30.1.1860: Launched by Brocklebank, Whitehaven (Yard No. 146) for T. and J. Brocklebank, Liverpool as VERONICA. Registered at Liverpool.
1874: Acquired by Anderson, Anderson and Co., London.
24.7.1874: Registered at London.
17.10.1879: Registered at Aberdeen.
25.6.1884: Sold to William Robertson, London.
8.2.1886: Foundered at Port Nolloth, South Africa after colliding with the barque MARQUIS OF WORCESTER (419/1861) during a south-easterly gale whilst on a voyage from Cape Town to Swansea with a cargo of copper ore.
1.4.1886: Register closed.

Two photographs of *Hesperus*. She and *Aurora* were the finest and largest ships in the Anderson fleet. After the loss of the one-year-old *Aurora* by fire in 1875, a slightly smaller replacement, *Harbinger,* was ordered from the Greenock shipbuilder Robert Steele. *[Above: Maritime Museum of Monterey; below: John Naylon collection]*

Hesperus and *Harbinger* were also the last sailing ships owned by the company and were sold to Devitt and Moore in 1890 as cadet ships. The photo above depicts *Harbinger* at Sydney whilst the view below is probably in a British port. Opposite we see her in the Alfred Graving Dock, Williamstown, Melbourne. *[Above and opposite: Maritime Museum of Monterey; below: National Maritime Museum 4793]*

AURORA 1874-1875 Iron ship. Australian trade.
O.N. 70640 1,857g 261.9 x 39.5 x 23.6 feet.
15.9.1874: Launched by Robert Steele and Co., Greenock (Yard No. 84).
16.10.1874: Registered at London in the ownership of Anderson, Anderson and Co., London as AURORA.
9.8.1875: On first return voyage from Adelaide with a cargo of wool, caught fire west of Azores in position 39 north by 37 west. She was abandoned and all 37 passengers and 47 crew were rescued by the ship MELMERBY (1,510/1863).

HARBINGER 1876-1890 Iron ship. Australian trade.
O.N. 73711 1,585g 253.5 x 37.6 x 22.4 feet.
Passengers: 30 first, 200 emigrants.
10.8.1876: Launched by Robert Steele and Co., Greenock (Yard No. 97).
15.9.1876: Registered at London in the ownership of Anderson, Anderson and Co., London as HARBINGER.
21.7.1880: Registered at Aberdeen.
28.4.1890: Sold to Devitt and Moore, London for use as a cadet ship.
1897: Sold to Johan Enlund, Raumo, Finland.
1.1910: Sold to Dutch buyers.
8.1910: Sold Maguiette, Antwerp for demolition at Hoboken.

Following the death of Captain William Perry in 1876, the seven ships owned by Thomas Bilbe and Co. were bought by Anderson, Anderson and Co. Within two years, four of the smaller ex-Bilbe ships had been sold.

Above: *White Eagle.*
[*Maritime Museum of Monterey*]

Left: *White Eagle* as *Pareora* at Port Chalmers in 1883.
[*Alexander Turnbull Library F-15441-1/2*]

WHITE EAGLE 1876 Iron ship.
O.N. 31755 879g 203.3 x 32.8 x 20.9 feet.
1855: Completed by A. Stephen and Sons, Glasgow (Yard No. 8).
23.3.1855: Registered at London in the ownership of A. Stephen and W.S. Croudace, Glasgow as WHITE EAGLE.
1856: Sold to John MacFarlane, Glasgow.
8.9.1860: Sold to A.G. Robinson, London.
1865: Sold to Thomas Bilbe and Co., London.
13.9.1865: Registered at London.
9.1876: Acquired by Anderson, Anderson and Co., London.
18.12.1876: Sold to the New Zealand Shipping Co. Ltd., London. Registered at Dunedin.
27.7.1877: Renamed PAREORA.
29.1.1878: Registered at London.
21.5.1879: Registered at Lyttelton.
28.12.1886: Registered at London.
19.2.1887: Sold to O.S. Piper, Port Talbot.
2.3.1888: Register closed after being broken up.

RED RIDING HOOD 1876-1878 Composite ship.
Australian/world-wide trade.
O.N. 20482 720g 183.2 x 29.6 x 19.7 feet.
25.8.1857: Completed by Thomas Bilbe and Co., Rotherhithe for their own account as RED RIDING HOOD. Designed for China tea trade, and the first Bilbe-built composite ship.
23.11.1857: Registered at London.

1876: Acquired by Anderson, Anderson and Co., London.
1878: Sold at Batavia to 'Arabs' (possibly Muslims from the Dutch East Indies) and renamed ISCANDRIA.
23.8.1878: Register closed. Reduced to barque rig.
1880: Sold to P. Landberg and and B.C. de Jong, Batavia and renamed BAREND-CHRISTIAAN. Probably used for the transportation of salt from Madura to various ports in the Dutch East Indies.
1890: Broken up locally.

ARGONAUT 1876-1883 Composite ship. Australian/world-wide trade.
O.N. 56727 1,073g 206.4 x 33.2 x 20.6 feet.
25.10.1866: Completed by Thomas Bilbe and Co., Rotherhithe for their own account as ARGONAUT.
16.11.1866: Registered at London.
1876: Acquired by Anderson, Anderson and Co., London.
21.10.1879: Registered at Aberdeen
7.1883: Sold to Jacob Brothers and Co., London and reduced to barque rig.
9.7.1883: Registered at London.
30.8.1888: Sold at auction in Port Natal after arriving, bound for Hamburg, in leaky state and condemned.
3.10.1888: Register closed.

Holmsdale. [Both: Maritime Museum of Monterey]

BOREALIS 1876-1884 Composite ship. Australian/world-wide trade.

O.N. 50063 920g 205.0 x 32 x 21.0 feet.

25.6.1864: Completed by Thomas Bilbe and Co., Rotherhithe for their own account as BOREALIS.

22.8.1864: Registered at London.

1876: Acquired by Anderson, Anderson and Co., London.

21.10.1879: Registered at Aberdeen.

1884: Sold to G. Brailli, Trieste (and later Orebich) Austria and renamed MARIETTA BRAILLI.

16.6.1884: Register closed.

9.1896: Reported as broken up.

HOLMSDALE 1876-1887 Wooden ship. Australian/world-wide trade.

O.N. 21590 1,352g 206.8 x 37.7 x 22.4 feet.

3.1858: Launched by William Briggs and Son, Sunderland.

31.5.1858: Registered at London in the ownership of William Phillips and Co., London as HOLMSDALE.

1874: Sold to Thomas Bilbe and Co., London.

1876: Acquired by Anderson, Anderson and Co., London.

18.10.1879: Registered at Aberdeen.

3.8.1887: Sold to G. Milne and Co., London.

19.3.1890: Register closed on sale to C. A. Jensen, Sarpsborg, Norway and renamed MYNT.

1894: Registered owner became 'Mynt' H. Jacobsen A/S.

7.1.1897: Sailed from Mobile, Alabama for Newcastle-on-Tyne and went missing.

WITCH OF THE WAVE 1876-1877 Wooden barque.
O.N. 5363 253g 113.1 x 22.2 x 15.4 feet.
20.6.1853: Completed by John Mansfield, Teignmouth for Thomas Hutchings, Teignmouth as WITCH OF THE WAVE.
1.8.1853: Registered at Teignmouth.
1868: Sold to Guthrie and Co., Liverpool.
21.2.1868: Registered at Liverpool.
1875: Sold to Thomas Bilbe and Co., London with her captain, Robert Guthrie, as registered owner.
1876: Acquired by Anderson, Anderson and Co., London with Robert Guthrie, managing owner.
13.8.1877: Wrecked at south east end of Choiseul Island, Solomon Islands whilst on a voyage from Kwo Kwo, Solomon Islands to Sydney with a cargo of island produce. The Annual Wreck Return shows owner as Cowlishaw Brothers, Sydney.
31.12.1877: Register closed.

GLEAM 1876-1877 Composite barque.
O.N. 27205 292g 141.1 x 21.8 x 14.2 feet.
1859: Completed by Thomas Bilbe and Co., London for their own account as GLEAM.
17.2.1859: Registered at London.
1876: Acquired by Anderson, Anderson and Co., London.
1877: Sold to William Robertson, London.
3.4.1882: Ran aground off Black Jack Rock, Port Nolloth, South Africa whilst waiting to enter port whilst on a voyage from Swansea to Port Nolloth with a cargo of coal and bags. Five lives were lost.
12.5.1882: Register closed.

ANGLO INDIAN 1878-1881 Wooden barque. West Indies trade.
O.N. 22181 444g 133.4 x 28.5 x 18.2 feet.
9.1858: Completed by J.M. Reed, Sunderland.
10.9.1858: Registered at London in the ownership of William Briggs, London as ANGLO INDIAN.
1864: Owner registered as Charles Briggs, Sunderland.
1869: Owner registered as A. Lambert, London.
1870: Owner registered as Henry Turner, London.
1873: Owner registered as George Slader, London.
1878: Acquired by Anderson, Anderson and Co., London.
10.10.1879: Registered at Aberdeen.
4.6.1881: Sold to Holme and Co., London.
1883: Sold to Frederick Ringer, Nagasaki.
5.3.1883: Registered at Shanghai.
4.1883: Sold to Peter V. Grant and J. Sharp, Shanghai.
1885: Sold to Nils Möller, Shanghai.
18.3.1893: Ownership transferred to Annie Möller, Shanghai.
20.6.1894: Register closed on sale to Chinese shipbreakers.

WOODBURN 1882-1896 Iron steam drogher. West Indies trade.
O.N. 52873 107g (1882: 143g 97n) 90.0 x 19.6 x 9.1 feet.
1882: C.2-cyl. by Pearce Brothers, Dundee; 18 NHP.
10.6.1865: Launched by A. Leslie and Co., Newcastle-upon-Tyne (Yard No. 65) as the iron sailing ship WOODBURN.
23.10.1865: Registered at Leith in the ownership of Donald McGregor, Leith.
1875: Sold to John Jordan, Leith.
1882: Acquired by Anderson, Anderson and Co., London and converted into a dandy-rigged screw drogher.
10.1882: Registered at London.
3.1896: Sold at auction in Montego Bay. Engines removed and hull abandoned.
25.3.1898: Register closed.

HEBBURN 1882-1896 Iron steam drogher. West Indies trade.
O.N. 52874 107g (1882: 144g 98n) 91.0 x 20.1 x 8.5 feet.
1882: C.2-cyl. by Plenty and Sons, Newbury; 18 NHP.
10.6.1865: Launched by A. Leslie and Co., Newcastle-upon-Tyne (Yard No. 66) as the iron sailing ship HEBBURN.
23.10.1865: Registered at Leith in the ownership of Donald McGregor, Leith.
1875: Sold to John Jordan, Leith.
1882: Acquired by Anderson, Anderson and Co., London and converted into a dandy-rigged screw drogher.
11.1882: Registered at London.
1896: Sold for scrap.

UNDINE 1882-1886 Iron steam drogher. West Indies trade.
O.N. 45659 155g 104n 116.5 x 19.5 x 8.9 feet.
C. 2-cyl. by William Simons and Co., Renfrew; 40 NHP.
15.1.1866: Launched by Kirkpatrick, McIntyre and Co., Port Glasgow (Yard No. 12).
27.6.1866: Registered at Bristol in the ownership of the Bristol General Steam Navigation Co., Bristol as UNDINE.
1871: Sold to John F. D'Oyle and Frederick J. Ransom, London.
14.3.1871: Registered at London.
7.7.1873: Sold to Edward Green, London.
5.3.1874: Sold to John Walsh and Richard Duckett, Preston.
3.11.1876: Sold to William Taylor, Birmingham.
23.12.1879: Sold to John White, London.
24.12.1879: Sold to John E. Kerr, Montego Bay, Jamaica.
10.9.1882: Acquired by Anderson, Anderson and Co., London.
1886: Broken up at Montego Bay.
30.12.1886: Register closed.

CARIB 1882-1896 Iron steamer. West Indies trade.
O.N. 84642 1,437g 912n 245.3 x 34.0 x 16.4 feet.
C.2-cyl. by Thomas Richardson and Sons, Hartlepool; 99 NHP.
28.9.1882: Launched by Richardson, Duck and Co., South Stockton (Yard No. 291).
31.10.1882: Registered at Stockton in the ownership of Anderson, Anderson and Co., London as CARIB.
20.10.1896: Sold to Maclay and McIntyre, Glasgow.
29.1.1897: Registered at Glasgow.
6.11.1897: Renamed IVANHOE. Registered owner now Steamship Ivanhoe Co. Ltd. (Maclay and McIntyre, managers), Glasgow.
24.4.1901: Register closed on sale to Memeler Dampschiffs A.G., Memel, Germany and renamed GERMANIA.
1904: Sold to Handelsb. Sölvesborg Skeppsvarf (J. Ingmansson, managers), Karlshamn, Sweden and renamed OTAGO.
10.6.1915: Sunk by the German submarine U 19, 30 miles east by north 25 north from Coquet Island, Northumberland whilst on a voyage from Umeå, Sweden to Hull with a cargo of timber.

MAROON (2) 1883-1896 Iron steamer. West Indies trade.
O.N. 87602 1,591g 1,029n 240.0 x 35.4 x 8.3 feet.
C. 2-cyl. by Day Summers and Co., Southampton; 135 NHP.
11.1.1883: Launched by Edward Finch Co. Ltd., Chepstow (Yard No. 34).
8.6.1883: Registered at Gloucester in the ownership of Anderson, Anderson and Co., London as MAROON.
20.10.1896: Sold to Maclay and McIntyre, Glasgow.
29.1.1897: Registered at Glasgow. Registered owner became Glasgow Navigation Co. Ltd. (Maclay and McIntyre, managers), Glasgow.
17.12.1910: Wrecked near Bayonne whilst on a voyage from Glasgow to Bayonne with a cargo of coal. One life was lost.
28.12.1910: Register closed.

COAL HULKS AT DIEGO GARCIA

ALCHYMIST 1886-1888 Wooden barque
O.N. 26865 540g 140.0 x 29.0 x 19.2 feet.
1859: Completed by R. Thompson, Sunderland (Yard No: 237) for Burnett and Co., Newcastle-upon-Tyne.
26.8.1864: Sold to Richard Jolly and Son, London.
1886: Acquired by Anderson, Anderson and Co., London for use as a coal hulk at Diego Garcia.
29.8.1887: Register closed
1888: Diego Garcia coaling station sold to William Lund and Son.

PETERBOROUGH 1866-1888 Wooden barque.
O.N. 26865 561g 138.0 x 29.0 x 19.2 feet.
8.1859: Completed by Austin and Mills, Sunderland for T. Hankey and Co., London.
1886: Acquired by Anderson, Anderson and Co., London for use as a coal hulk at Diego Garcia.
1888: Diego Garcia coaling station sold to William Lund and Son.

Note: the Pacific Steam Navigation Company also provided two coal hulks, RONOCHAN (O.N. 32921) 1,156/1849 and ARRAN (O.N. 47585) 962/1851).

SHIPS OF THE ORIENT LINE
JOINT SERVICE 1878-1909

Dates given after name show period of ownership by The Orient Steam Navigation Co. Ltd.
(1900: Orient Steam Navigation Co. Ltd.) or the period of employment on the joint Orient Line service to Australia
with the Pacific Steam Navigation Company, which lasted until 1906, and the Orient-Royal Mail Line 1906 to 1909.
All are steel single-screw steamers unless specified.

LUSITANIA 1878-1900 Iron
O.N. 65888 3,825g 2,420n 379.9 x 41.3 x 35.2 feet.
C.2-cyl. by Laird Brothers, Birkenhead; 550 NHP, 13 knots.
1886: T.3-cyl. by Thomas Richardson and Sons, Hartlepool; 700 NHP, 15 knots.
Passengers: 74 first, 76 second, 265 third (Australian service).
20.6.1871: Launched by Laird Brothers, Birkenhead (Yard No. 381).
26.9.1871: Registered at Liverpool in the ownership of the Pacific Steam Navigation Company, Liverpool as LUSITANIA.
29.9.1871: Left on maiden voyage from Birkenhead to Valparaiso.
9.4.1874: Arrived Birkenhead and laid up apart from one round voyage to South America, *15.12.1875* to *16.4.1876.*
1877: Chartered by Anderson, Anderson and Co. and Frederick Green and Co., London.
26.6.1877: Left on first voyage from London to Australia.
8.8.1877: Arrived Melbourne.
5.1878: Acquired by The Orient Steam Navigation Co. Ltd., London.

1.8.1882-16.2.1883: Chartered as a transport during Egyptian Campaign.
4.1885: Chartered for six months by Admiralty as armed merchant cruiser during Russian war scare.
6.2.1886-1.5.1886: Re-engined by Thomas Richardson and Sons, Hartlepool. Yards and topgallants on fore and main masts and third class accommodation removed.
1890s: Used extensively for cruising.
5.3.1900: After 35 mail voyages and 21 cruises, sold to Alfred Jones (Elder Dempster and Co.), Liverpool for use on the Beaver Line service to Canada.
25.7.1900: Sold to the Pacific Steam Navigation Company, Liverpool.
6.2.1901: Sold to Alfred Jones (Elder, Dempster and Co.), Liverpool.
26.6.1901: Wrecked at Seal Cove, 25 miles north of Cape Race, whilst on a voyage from Liverpool to Montreal on charter to Allan Line.
20.7.1901: Register closed.

Above: A pre-1886 view of the *Lusitania* off Tilbury.
[*F.C. Gould photo, Peter Newall collection*]

Right: *Lusitania* in later days on the River Mersey in Beaver Line colours.
[*J. and M. Clarkson collection*]

CHIMBORAZO 1878-1894 Iron

O.N. 65886 3,847g 2,443n 384.0 x 41.3 x 35.3 feet.
C.2-cyl. by John Elder and Co., Govan; 550 NHP, 13 knots.
Passengers: 72 first, 92 second, 265 third (Australian service).
21.6.1871: Launched by John Elder and Co., Govan (Yard No. 128).
19.9.1871: Registered at Liverpool in the ownership of the Pacific Steam Navigation Company, Liverpool as CHIMBORAZO.
13.10.1871: Left on maiden voyage from Birkenhead to Valparaiso.
28.7.1874: Arrived Birkenhead and laid up.
1877: Chartered by Anderson, Anderson and Co. and Frederick Green and Co., London.
12.8.1877: Left on first voyage from London to Australia.
15.3.1878: In thick fog, struck rocks at Point Perpendicular, near Jervis Bay. Passengers transferred to paddle steamer COLLAROY (356/1853). After temporary repairs, reached Sydney 31.3.1878.

14.6.1878: Repairs completed.
8.1878: Acquired by The Orient Steam Navigation Co. Ltd., London.
10.2.1880: Suffered severe storm damage in Bay of Biscay. One passenger and three seamen were washed overboard.
1890s: Used extensively for cruising.
9.10.1894: After 22 mail voyages and 19 cruises, sold to Frederick Joseph Pilcher, Liverpool for use as a cruise ship.
12.1.1895: Renamed CLEOPATRA.
22.3.1895: Registered owner became the Ocean Cruising and Highland Yachting Co. Ltd. (A.J. Turner, manager), Liverpool. Laid up at Birkenhead.
5.2.1897: Sold to Thomas W. Ward, Preston for breaking up.
21.3.1897: Arrived at Preston.
27.8.1897: Register closed.

Chimborazo photographed in the Thames before 1894 by F.C. Gould of Gravesend. *[Ian Farquhar collection]*

Cuzco before being modified in 1887. *[Peter Newall collection]*

CUZCO 1878-1905 Iron
O.N. 65901 3,845g 2,437n 384.2 x 41.4 x 35.3 feet.
C.2-cyl. by John Elder and Co., Govan; 550 NHP, 13 knots.
1888: T.3-cyl. by Fairfield Shipbuilding and Engineering Co. Ltd., Govan; 650 NHP, 15 knots.
Passengers: 74 first, 76 second, 265 third (Australian service).
18.10.1871: Launched by John Elder and Co., Govan (Yard No. 129).
20.12.1871: Registered at Liverpool in the ownership of the Pacific Steam Navigation Company, Liverpool as CUZCO.
13.1.1872: Left on maiden voyage from Birkenhead to Valparaiso.
28.3.1874: Arrived Birkenhead and laid up.
1877: Chartered by Anderson, Anderson and Co. and Frederick Green and Co., London.
25.9.1877: Left on first voyage from London to Australia.
3.1878: Acquired by The Orient Steam Navigation Co. Ltd., London.
17.8.1887-21.1.1888: Re-engined by Fairfield Shipbuilding and Engineering Co. Ltd., Govan. Yards and topgallants on fore and main masts and third class accommodation removed and funnel heightened.
20.1.1905: After 60 mail voyages, sold to Luigi Pittaluga, Genoa, Italy for demolition at Genoa.
28.1.1905: Register closed.
3.1905: Broken up.

GARONNE (1) 1878-1897 Iron
O.N. 65855 3,871g 2,468n 382.1 x 41.4 x 35.7
C. 2-cyl. by Robert Napier and Sons, Glasgow; 624 NHP, 13 knots.
Passengers: 70 first, 86 second, 265 third (Australian service).
22.4.1871: Launched by Robert Napier and Sons, Glasgow (Yard No. 152).
14.6.1871: Registered at Liverpool in the ownership of the Pacific Steam Navigation Company, Liverpool as GARONNE.
29.6.1871: Left on maiden voyage from Birkenhead to Valparaiso.
12.2.1878: Acquired by The Orient Steam Navigation Co. Ltd., London.
5.3.1878: Left on first voyage from London to Australia.
30.3.1878: Made first Orient Line call at Cape Town.
19.3.1879: After leaving Adelaide stranded on Tapley Shoal. Released after two days with help from two tugs.
1881: Given new boilers by Laird Bros., Birkenhead.
1890s: Used extensively for cruising.
11.1897: After 25 mail and 41 various voyages sold to John Porter, Liverpool.
1898: Sold to Frank Waterhouse Ltd. (John M. Mitchell, manager), London.
5.6.1898: Arrived at Victoria, British Columbia. Used in the Alaskan Gold Rush and as a troopship between San Francisco and the Philippines during the American-Spanish War.
28.7.1900: Register closed following sale to Frank Waterhouse, Seattle and registration under the United States flag.
11.1905: Broken up at Genoa.

Cuzco in the Thames after being re-engined in 1887/8. The funnel has been made taller to improve draught for the boilers and the yards removed. *[F.C. Gould photo, Ian Farquhar collection]*

Garonne (1) with yards removed moored in the Thames. *[F.C.Gould photo, Ian Farquhar collection]*

ACONCAGUA 1878-1881 Iron

O.N. 65969 4,106g 2,639n 404.8 x 41.4 x 35.3 feet.
C.2-cyl. by John Elder and Co., Govan; 600 NHP, 13 knots.
Passengers: 126 first, 40 second, 800 third.
6.6.1872: Launched by John Elder and Co., Govan (Yard No. 130).
16.9.1872: Registered at Liverpool in the ownership of the Pacific Steam Navigation Company, Liverpool as ACONCAGUA.
28.9.1872: Left on maiden voyage from Birkenhead to Valparaiso.
17.5.1878: Left on first voyage from London to Australia.
11.5.1881: Left on final sailing to Australia.
28.2.1895: Register closed on sale to Verdeau et Compagnie, Bordeaux, France and renamed EGYPTE.
1896: Sold for scrap in France.

JOHN ELDER 1879-1886 Iron

O.N. 63313 3,832g 2,431n 381.9 x 41.5 x 35.2 feet.
1873: 4,152g 2,651n 406.4 x 41.5 x 35.2 feet.
C.2-cyl. by John Elder and Co., Govan; 550 NHP, 12 knots.
Passengers: 72 first, 92 second, 265 third.
29.8.1870: Launched by John Elder and Co., Govan (Yard No. 110).
9.11.1870: Registered at Liverpool in the ownership of the Pacific Steam Navigation Company, Liverpool as JOHN ELDER.
13.12.1870: Left on maiden voyage from Birkenhead to Valparaiso.
1872-3: Lengthened and given second funnel.
4.1874: Caught fire in dry dock at Birkenhead.
5.1876: Returned to service.
27.1.1879: Left on first voyage from London to Australia.
27.5.1886: Left on final sailing to Australia.
16.1.1892: Wrecked in fog on the Cavausa Rocks off Cape Carranza, Chile whilst on a voyage from Valparaiso to Talcahuano.
29.3.1892: Register closed.

Aconcagua at Tilbury in May 1879. *[National Maritime Museum G.1504]*

John Elder off Tilbury after lengthening and having her second funnel fitted. *[National Maritime Museum G.2335]*

Sorata off Tilbury. *[National Maritime Museum G.1594]*

SORATA 1880-1886 Iron

O.N. 65991 4,014g 2,573n 401.3 x 42.8 x 34.1 feet.
C.2-cyl. by John Elder and Co., Govan; 600 NHP, 12 knots.
Passengers: 140 first, 50 second, 800 third.
2.10.1872: Launched by John Elder and Co., Govan (Yard No. 144).
20.12.1872: Registered at Liverpool in the ownership of the Pacific Steam Navigation Company, Liverpool as SORATA.
8.1.1873: Left on maiden voyage from Birkenhead to Valparaiso.
13.2.1880: Left on first voyage from London to Australia.
3.9.1880: Stranded on Yatala Shoal, Backstairs Passage, South Australia.
13.11.1880: Refloated and towed to Semaphore Anchorage, Adelaide.
3.1880-21.6.1881: In drydock at Melbourne for repairs.
29.4.1886: Left on final sailing to Australia.
28.10.1895: Sold to E. Thirkell and Co., Liverpool.
12.1895: Demolished at Tranmere.
7.5.1897: Register closed.

COTOPAXI 1880-1882 Iron

O.N. 69265 4,028g 2,583n 402.2 x 42.8 x 34.3 feet.
C.2-cyl. by John Elder and Co., Govan; 600 NHP, 12 knots.
Passengers: 136 first, 41 second, 800 third.
15.3.1873: Launched by John Elder and Co., Govan (Yard No. 146).
26.5.1873: Registered at Liverpool in the ownership of the Pacific Steam Navigation Company, Liverpool as COTOPAXI.
18.6.1873: Left on maiden voyage from Birkenhead to Valparaiso.
25.9.1873: Grounded on reef near Bahia. Refloated two days later.
15.3.1874: Arrived Liverpool and laid up apart from one round voyage to South America, *10.12.1879 to 25.2.1880.*
14.4.1880: Left on first voyage from London to Australia.
28.12.1882: Left on final sailing to Australia.
8.4.1889: Collided with OLYMPIA and beached near Cape Forward in Straits of Magellan whilst on a voyage from Birkenhead to Valparaiso.
11.4.1889: Refloated.
15.4.1889: Foundered after striking uncharted rock in Messier Channel. All passengers and crew were saved.
15.6.1889: Register closed.

Sorata stranded on Yatala Shoal in 1880. *[Peter Newall collection]*

Cotopaxi in the Thames April 1880 before her first voyage to Australia.
[National Maritime Museum G.2157]

An artist's impression of the loss of *Cotopaxi* in the Straits of Magellan. *[Peter Newall collection]*

LIGURIA 1880-1890 Iron

O.N. 69367 4,666g 2,980n 433.4 x 45.0 x 34.1 feet.
C. 3-cyl. by John Elder and Co., Govan; 750 NHP, 4,000 IHP, 13 knots.
1893: Engines tripled by D. Rollo and Sons, Liverpool; 15 knots.
Passengers: 100 first, 150 second, 340 third.
18.2.1874: Launched by John Elder and Co., Govan (Yard No. 161).
28.5.1874: Registered at Liverpool in the ownership of the Pacific Steam Navigation Company, Liverpool as LIGURIA.
9.9.1874: Left on maiden voyage from Birkenhead to Valparaiso.
12.5.1880: Left on first voyage from London to Australia.
6.5.1890: Left on final sailing to Australia.
1893: Engines converted to triple expansion, yards on fore and main masts removed.
1903: Sold to F. Bruzzo, Genoa, Italy.
12.1903: Broken up at Genoa.
14.8.1903: Register closed.

POTOSI 1880-1887 Iron screw

O.N. 69278 4,219n 2,704g 421.6 x 43.3 x 33.5 feet.
C.2-cyl. by John Elder and Co., Govan; 600 NHP, 13 knots.
Passengers: 136 first, 41 second, 800 third.
14.5.1873: Launched by John Elder and Co., Govan (Yard No. 157).
5.7.1873: Registered at Liverpool in the ownership of the Pacific Steam Navigation Company, Liverpool as POTOSI.

6.8.1873: Left on maiden voyage from Birkenhead to Valparaiso.
7.7.1880: Left on first voyage from London to Australia.
26.5.1887: Left on final sailing to Australia.
1897: Sold to Italian breakers at Genoa.
11.6.1897: Register closed.
7.1897: Broken up.

IBERIA 1883-1890 Iron

O.N. 69336 4,671g 2,982n 433.5 x 45.0 x 34.1 feet.
C. 3-cyl. by John Elder and Co., Govan; 750 NHP, 13 knots.
1893: Tripled by D. Rollo and Sons, Liverpool; 15 knots.
Passengers: 140 first, 50 second, 800 third.
6.12.1873: Launched by John Elder and Co., Govan (Yard No. 162).
16.2.1874: Registered at Liverpool in the ownership of the Pacific Steam Navigation Company, Liverpool as IBERIA.
21.10.1874: Left on maiden voyage from Birkenhead to Valparaiso.
24.7-16.12.1882: Chartered as a transport during Egyptian Campaign.
25.1.1883: Left on first voyage from London to Australia.
2.1889: Made first Orient Line call at Colombo.
31.1.1890: Left on final sailing to Australia.
1893: Engines converted to triple expansion.
6.4.1903: Register closed on sale to F. Bruzzo, Genoa, Italy.
5.1903: Broken up at Genoa.

Liguria photographed by F.C. Gould off Tilbury on 17th August 1888 (above) and in the Mersey with her yards removed (right).
[Above: National Maritime Museum G.634 and right: Peter Newall collection]

Potosi at Tilbury on 29th October 1885.   *[National Maritime Museum G.1613]*

Iberia off Tilbury in June 1889. At the time of her completion, she was the largest ship in the world after *Great Eastern*.
[National Maritime Museum G.147]

ORIENT (2) 1879-1910 Iron

O.N. 82254 5,365g 3,231n 445.6 x 46.3 x 35.1 feet..
C. 3-cyl. by John Elder and Co., Govan 1,000 NHP 15 knots.
1898: T. 3-cyl. by Wallsend Slipway and Engineering Co. Ltd., Wallsend-on-Tyne; 1,100 NHP, 8,200 IHP, 16 knots.
Passengers: 120 first, 130 second, 300 third.
Refrigerated space: 35,113 cubic feet.
5.6.1879: Launched by John Elder and Co., Govan (Yard No. 224).
5.9.1879: Registered at Glasgow in the ownership of The Orient Steam Navigation Co. Ltd., London as ORIENT.
1.11.1879: Left on first voyage from London to Australia, during which she reduced the London to Adelaide record to 37 days 22 hours.

1880: On second outbound voyage, reduced the Plymouth to Cape Town record to 17 days 21 hours - this was unbroken for ten years.
23.7-20.9.1882: Chartered as a transport during Egyptian Campaign.
1880s: Given turtleback poop and topgallant-forecastle. Her yards were also later removed.
19.12.1897-6.4.1898: New engine installed and masts reduced from four to two, and twin funnels replaced with a single tall one.
13.10.1899-10.11.1902: Boer War Transport No. 24.
11.1.1910: After 66 mail and trooping voyages, sold to Luigi Pittaluga, Genoa, Italy for demolition at Genoa.
15.1.1910: Register closed.
3.10.1910: Arrived at Genoa as ORIC.

Orient (2) in various ports and guises:

Opposite page top: In the Thames as built, with yards and flush deck. She was then the largest ship in the world after *Great Eastern*.
[Ian Farquhar collection]

Opposite page bottom: Photographed at Melbourne prior to 1897 by Charles Rudd. In the late 1880s/early 1890s her yards were removed and a topgallant-forecastle and raised poop added.
[Ian Farquhar collection]

Top: Outward bound from Sydney as seen by William Livermore. Two smaller funnels have been replaced by one tall funnel and two masts removed.
[Ian Farquhar collection]

Middle: As Boer War Transport No. 24 perhaps at Southampton.
[Peter Newall collection]

Bottom: Post 1906, off Tilbury, now sporting the yellow Orient Line funnel.
[Peter Newall collection]

AUSTRAL 1882-1903

O.N. 85923 5,589g 3,271n 456 x 48.2 x 33.9 feet.
C. 3-cyl. by John Elder and Co., Govan; 1,000 NHP, 17 knots.
Passengers: 120 first, 130 second, 300 third (*1884:* 136 first, 174 second, 300 third).
Refrigerated space: 57,791 cubic feet.
24.12.1881: Launched by John Elder and Co., Govan (Yard No. 249).
27.4.1882: Registered at Glasgow in the ownership of The Orient Steam Navigation Co. Ltd., London as AUSTRAL.
19.5.1882: Left on maiden voyage from London to Australia.
11.11.1882: Sank during coaling at Sydney. Five of the crew drowned.
1.3.1883: Refloated.
9.6.1883: Sailed from Sydney in ballast for Glasgow via Cape Horn.

8.1883: Arrived on the Clyde.
1884: After rebuilding, which probably included the removal of yards from fore and main masts, placed on Anchor Line's Liverpool to New York service for seven round voyages between 19.4.1884 and 4.10.1884.
26.5.1885: Reduced the London to Melbourne record to 35 days 4 hours.
Late 1890s: Funnels raised by 16 feet with extension pieces smaller in diameter than original funnels.
9.2.1900 to *26.4.1900:* Chartered as a Boer War transport.
5.1903: After 53 mail voyages, sold to Italian breakers Gastaldi, Genoa.
7.5.1903: Register closed.
27.5.1903: Arrived Genoa.
9.1905: Broken up.

Above: *Austral,* as built, photographed by F.C. Gould in the Thames at Tilbury.
[*National Maritime Museum G.649*]

Right: *Austral* after sinking whilst coaling at Sydney. [*Peter Newall collection*] A series of photographs of the salvage operation appear on pages 62 and 63.

Austral in 1895 at Tilbury - the yards have gone but the funnels remain as built. *[National Maritime Museum G.1123]*

Austral in the Thames after her funnels have been extended. *[National Maritime Museum G.1122]*

Refloating *Austral* involved constructing a wooden cofferdam around the ship. The photographs opposite give an idea of the massive task involved with timber supports, pulleys, pipes and pumps.
[National Maritime Museum C7962/10, 12, 2 and 5]

On 27th February 1883 with the cofferdam complete, pumping commenced (left). Three days later on 1st March *Austral* was afloat and the cofferdam can be clearly seen (below). After three months in dry dock, *Austral* left Sydney under her own steam on 9th June.
[National Maritime Museum C.7962/8 and 1]

Escort with passengers at the Landing Stage of the Town Jetty in Albany, Western Australia. [Albany Historical Society Inc.]

Camilla early in her career as a schooner.

ESCORT 1884-1900 Iron tug
O.N. 89597 28g 7n 49.6 x 12.6 x 7.0 feet.
C.2-cyl. by J. Stewart and Son, Blackwall; 20 NHP.
1884: Completed by R. and H. Green, Blackwall (Yard No. 476).
16.7.1884: Registered at London in the ownership of The Orient Steam Navigation Co. Ltd., London and the Pacific Steam Navigation Company, Liverpool for the Diego Garcia coaling station as ESCORT.
1888: Diego Garcia coaling station sold to William Lund and Son.
1889: Moved to Albany, Western Australia. Operated with lighter CAMILLA.
11.12.1900: Sold to Alexander Armstrong Senior, Albany, Western Australia.
16.1.1901: Registered at Fremantle.
18.10.1903: Wrecked at Nornalup Inlet, 60 miles west of Albany, Western Australia: 35.01 south by 116.44 east. Much of the wreck is still intact including engine and boiler.
6.10.1913: Register closed.

ESTRELLA 1886-1912 Wooden lugger-rigged steam tug/launch
O.N. 89313 46g 31n 71.6 x 15.6 x 6.6 feet.
C.2-cyl. by Plenty and Sons, Newbury; 25 NHP.
6.11.1884: Launched by William Dunn, North Shore, Sydney.
10.12.1884: Registered at Sydney in the ownership of Henry Perdriau Junior, Balmain, Sydney as ESTRELLA. (Henry Perdriau was a local ferry operator.)
19.5.1886: Sold to Arthur Adair, Devon, England who turned out to be a confidence trickster posing as Sir Arthur Adair.
9.9.1886: Acquired by The Orient Steam Navigation Co. Ltd., London and registered in name of Thomas Pugh, Assistant Manager, Orient Line, Sydney. Remained in his name until 1912 despite his death on 11.11.1889.
25.1.1912: Sold to John Horn, Sydney.
20.8.1928: Sold to Percy Jacobsen, Sydney.
7.1933: Broken up at Sydney.
5.4.1934: Registered closed.

CAMILLA 1891-1903 Wooden lighter
O.N. 32403 201g 85.9 x 23.6 x 14.5 feet.
1834: Completed as a schooner by Robert Menzie and Son, Leith.
21.3.1834: Registered at Leith in the ownership of the London and Leith Old Shipping Company (founded in 1812) as CAMILLA.
25.5.1848: Sold to Ninian Lockhart, Kirkaldy and registered at Kirkaldy.
27.5.1851: Sold to Frederick Lipscombe, Hobart Town, Tasmania and registered at Hobart.
11.6.1851: Sold to Charles Hartam, Hobart Town.
24.6.1853: Sold to Peter Finlay, Twofold Bay, New South Wales and registered at Sydney.
9.9.1861: Sold to John Clinch, Hobart Town and re-registered at Hobart. Sometime later the managing owner was William Belbin, a Tasmanian timber merchant.
1890: Owned by the Bank of Van Dieman's Land Ltd., Hobart.
26.3.1891: Sold to The Orient Steam Navigation Co. Ltd., London.
10.9.1891: Registered at London. Transferred to Albany, Western Australia and after removal of masts (new tonnage 190.3g) used as a lighter towed by ESCORT.
12.1900: Laid up after sale of ESCORT and later sold to J. Ball who moved her to Fremantle.
24.2.1903: Condemned and ordered by the Fremantle Harbour Trust to be removed as she was an obstruction. She was beached beyond Woodman Point.
14.4.1903: Register closed.

ORMUZ (1) 1886-1912
O.N. 93341 6,031g 2,940n 465.5 x 52.1 x 34.1 feet.
T.3-cyl. by Fairfield Shipbuilding and Engineering Co. Ltd., Glasgow; 1,400 NHP, 9,000 IHP, 18 knots.
Passengers: 168 first, 168 second, 300 third.
Refrigerated space: 44,501 cubic feet.
29.9.1886: Launched by Fairfield Shipbuilding and Engineering Co. Ltd., Glasgow (Yard No. 317).
29.12.1886: Registered at Glasgow in the ownership of The Orient Steam Navigation Co. Ltd., London as ORMUZ.
3.2.1887: Left on maiden voyage from London to Australia.
10.12.1900: Badly damaged in collision with the steamer ISMAILA (5,265/1900) whilst entering Melbourne.
31.1.1901. Sailed from Melbourne after repairs to her bow. Funnels heightened around this time.
10.4.1912: After 70 mail voyages, sold to Compagnie de Navigation Sud Atlantique, Bordeaux, France and renamed DIVONA.
17.5.1912: Register closed.
19.10.1912: Left on first voyage from Bordeaux to South America.
5.12.1915: Requisitioned by French Government and converted at Toulon into a 600-bed hospital ship.
1.4.1918: Returned to owners but was again requisitioned for trooping duties.
3.1920: Returned to owners.
11.6.1922: Arrived at Marseilles under tow for dismantling. Demolition completed during third quarter of 1922, possibly at Savona.

Ormuz (1) as built, at Sydney. *[National Maritime Museum G.1587]*

Ormuz (1) with her yards removed and the Gravesend to Tilbury ferry/tender *Thames* (125/1868) alongside.
[National Maritime Museum G.134]

A William Livermore view of *Ormuz* (1) outbound from Sydney in July 1904 after her funnels had been heightened. *[Ian Farquhar collection]*

Orizaba in the Thames with yards and funnels as built.
[*National Maritime Museum G.1593*]

ORIZABA 1886-1905

O.N. 93688 6,184g 3,587n 460.0 x 49.3 x 19.4 feet.
T.3-cyl. by the Barrow Shipbuilding Co. Ltd., Barrow-in-Furness; 1,200 NHP, 7,000 IHP, 16.5 knots.
Passengers: 126 first, 154 second, 412 third.
Refrigerated space: 44,500 cubic feet.
6.5.1886: Launched by the Barrow Shipbuilding Co. Ltd., Barrow-in-Furness (Yard No. 138).
31.8.1886: Registered at Liverpool in the ownership of the Pacific Steam Navigation Company, Liverpool as ORIZABA.
30.9.1886: Left on maiden voyage from London to Australia.
1890s: Yards removed and funnels heightened.
24.11.1898: Registered at London.
17.2.1905: Ran aground near Fremantle on Five Fathom Bank between Point Peron and Garden Island in smoke haze caused by bush fires whilst outward bound to Sydney. Declared a constructive total loss.
5.6.1906: Register closed.

OROYA 1887-1909

O.N. 93712 6,057g 3,266n 460.0 x 49.3 x 35.3 feet.
T.3-cyl. by Barrow Shipbuilding Company, Barrow-in-Furness; 1,200 NHP, 7,000 IHP, 16.5 knots.
Passengers: 126 first, 154 second, 412 third.
Refrigerated space: 44,500 cubic feet.
31.8.1886: Launched by Barrow Shipbuilding Company, Barrow-in-Furness (Yard No. 139).
12.1.1887: Registered at Liverpool in the ownership of the Pacific Steam Navigation Company, Liverpool as OROYA.
17.2.1887: Left on maiden voyage from London to Australia.
4.3.1895: Ran ashore near Naples.
23.4.1895: Refloated and towed to Naples.
24.5.1895: Arrived at Belfast for repairs.
29.10.1895: Left London for Australia.
1890s: Funnels heightened.
2.1906: Sold to Royal Mail Steam Packet Company, London. Masts reduced from four to three.
10.1909: With the end of the Orient-Royal Mail Steam Packet Company joint service, sold to Italian shipbreakers F. Bruzzo, Genoa.
30.10.1909: Register closed.
15.11.1909: Arrived at Genoa as ORO under Italian flag.
12.1909: Broken up.

Oroya in her original state.
[*Peter Newall collection*]

Above: *Oroya* aground near Naples in 1895.
[National Maritime Museum G.1817]

Right: *Oroya* with funnels heightened.
[National Maritime Museum G.4]

Below: *Oroya* in the ownership of the Royal Mail Steam Packet Company Limited. The mainmast has been removed.
[National Maritime Museum G.1131]

OROTAVA 1890-1909

O.N. 96348 5,552g 3,096n 430.0 x 49.3 x 34.2 feet.
T.3-cyl. by the Naval Construction and Armament Co. Ltd., Barrow-in-Furness; 1,030 NHP, 7,000 IHP, 16 knots.
Passengers: 126 first, 120 second, 400 third.
Refrigerated space: about 40,000 cubic feet.
15.6.1889: Launched by the Naval Construction and Armament Co. Ltd., Barrow-in-Furness (Yard No. 166).
15.8.1889: Registered at Liverpool in the ownership of the Pacific Steam Navigation Company, Liverpool as OROTAVA.
16.10.1889: Left on maiden voyage from Birkenhead to Valparaiso.
6.6.1890: Left on first voyage from London to Australia.
1890s: Funnels heightened.
14.12.1896: Sank whilst coaling at Tilbury. Four lives were lost. Raised a week later.
2.1897: Returned to service.

13.2.1900-31.12.1902: Boer War Transport No. 91.
16.1.1906: Sold to Royal Mail Steam Packet Company, London.
1.2.1906: Registered at London. Masts reduced from four to two.
5.3.1909: Left on final voyage from London to Australia. Placed on Royal Mail Steam Packet Company's West Indies service.
11.1914: Requisitioned by Admiralty for use as an armed merchant cruiser.
30.9.1915: Sold to the Admiralty (Royal Mail Steam Packet Company, managers).
17.12.1914: Commissioned as HMS OROTAVA in the Tenth Cruiser Squadron.
1.1.1919: Paid off.
25.2.1919: Registered at London in the ownership of the Shipping Controller. Used as a troopship.
1921: Broken up on the Clyde in fourth quarter.
23.2.1923: Register closed.

Right: *Orotava* photographed by F.C. Gould on 13th February 1891 as built. [National Maritime Museum G.1154]

Below: *Orotava* being righted in Tilbury Docks after sinking in December 1896 whilst coaling. *[National Maritime Museum G.148]*

Top: *Orotava* in the Thames as Boer War
Transport No. 91. Funnels have been
heightened.

[*Peter Newall collection*]

Middle: *Orotava* in Royal Mail Steam Packet
Company colours in January 1907. Two
masts have been removed.

[*National Maritime Museum G.103*]

Right: As the armed merchant cruiser *HMS
Orotava*. [*Ships in Focus collection*]

ORUBA 1890-1905

O.N. 96310 5,552g 3,096n 430.0 x 49.3 x 34.2 feet.
T.3-cyl. by the Naval Construction and Armaments Co. Ltd., Barrow-in-Furness; 1,030 NHP, 7,000 IHP, 16 knots.
Passengers: 126 first, 120 second, 400 third.
Refrigerated space: about 40,000 cubic feet.
20.3.1889: Launched by Naval Construction and Armaments Co. Ltd., Barrow-in-Furness (Yard No. 165).
22.5.1889: Registered at Liverpool in the ownership of the Pacific Steam Navigation Company, Liverpool as ORUBA.

26.6.1889: Left on maiden voyage from Birkenhead to Valparaiso.
4.7.1890: Left on first voyage from London to Australia.
1890s: Funnels heightened.
2.1906: Sold to Royal Mail Steam Packet Company, London. Masts reduced from four to two.
28.10.1914: Sold to the Admiralty. Converted by Harland and Wolff Ltd., Belfast into dummy battleship HMS ORION.
2.10.1915: Register closed.
1.1.1916: Scuttled as a breakwater extension in Kephalo Bay on the Aegean island, Imbros.

Oruba, photographed with extended funnels (above) and in Royal Mail colours (below) after the removal of two masts. The vessel alongside in the upper photo is *Tilbury* (269/1883) owned by the London, Tilbury and Southend Railway Company.
[National Maritime Museum G.744 and G.1048]

Oruba at Scapa Flow in June 1915 after being transformed into *HMS Orion* - a dummy battleship (above).
A broadside view of *HMS Orion* (right).
Her dummy wooden guns are shown below.
In January 1916 *HMS Orion* was scuttled at Kephalo Bay to form a breakwater against the fierce north westerly gales from which she suffered badly (bottom right).

[Top, right and bottom right, Imperial War Museum SP.533, S.P.15, Q.13,638; below: Maritime Photo Library]

OPHIR 1891-1918 Twin screw
O.N. 98673 6,910g 3,223n 465.0 x 53.4 x 34.1 feet.
Two T.3-cyl. by Robert Napier and Sons, Glasgow; 1,734 NHP, 10,000 IHP, 18 knots.
Passengers: 222 first, 150 second, 500 third.
Refrigerated space: 52,400 cubic feet.
11.4.1891: Launched by Robert Napier and Sons, Glasgow (Yard No. 421).
31.10.1891: Registered at Glasgow in the ownership of The Orient Steam Navigation Co. Ltd., London as OPHIR.
6.11.1891: Left on maiden voyage from London to Australia. She was the first twin-screw passenger ship running to Australia.
1901: Chartered as royal yacht for a tour of the colonies by the Duke and Duchess of Cornwall and York (later King George V and Queen Mary) from 16th March to 1st November.
26.2.1901: Commissioned as HMS OPHIR after conversion at Tilbury.
5.2.1915: After 51 mail voyages, sold to Admiralty for use as an armed merchant cruiser.
3.3.1915: Commissioned as HMS OPHIR.
6.1917: Paid off at Liverpool.
2.1918: Re-commissioned.
11.2.1919: Paid off and laid up on the Clyde.
8.1921: Sold for scrap.
1922: Broken up at Troon.

Ophir on trials (top); arriving back in Portsmouth 1st November 1901 after the royal tour (middle) and as *HMS Ophir,* an armed merchant cruiser (right).
[Top: Glasgow University Archives DC101/0461.(X2); middle and lower National Maritime Museum G.4133 and unnumbered] Interior views of her as a royal yacht appear on pages 156-157.

Between March and November 1901 *Ophir* was used as a royal yacht and toured most of the British Empire with the Duke and Duchess of Cornwall and York (later King George V and Queen Mary).

Above left: Duke and Duchess of Cornwall and York seen with the Earl of Athlone alongside *Ophir* at Halifax on 20th October. *[P&O Archives PO-1-4701]*

Above right: Whilst the royal couple went on a month-long tour of Canada from 16th September to 19th October, *Ophir* was dry docked at Halifax, Nova Scotia for cleaning and painting. *[National Maritime Museum P3036]*

Below: *Ophir* returning to Portsmouth 1st November with HMS *Victory* in the background. *[Ambrose Greenway collection]*

OMRAH 1899-1918 Twin screw
O.N. 108782 8,291g 4,632n 490.7 x 56.7 x 34.2 feet.
Two T.3-cyl. by Fairfield Shipbuilding and Engineering Co. Ltd.,
Glasgow; 1,350 NHP, 9,200 IHP, 18 knots.
Passengers: 161 first, 162 second, 500 third.
Refrigerated space: 77,000 cubic feet.
3.9.1898: Launched by Fairfield Shipbuilding and Engineering Co.
Ltd., Glasgow (Yard No: 404).
29.12.1898: Registered at Glasgow in the ownership of The Orient
Steam Navigation Co. Ltd., London as OMRAH.

3.2.1899: Left on maiden voyage from London to Australia.
9.1914-2.1915: Chartered as a troop transport by the Australian
Government.
4.1917: Requisitioned under the Liner Requisition Scheme as a
troop transport.
12.5.1918: Torpedoed by the German submarine UB 52, 60 miles
south west of Cape Spartivento, Sardinia, whilst on a voyage from
Marseilles to Alexandria with mail. One life was lost.
19.6.1918: Register closed.

Omrah sailing from Sydney (above) and sailing from Melbourne on 17th January 1917 (right).

[Above: Ian Farquhar collection right: J. and M. Clarkson collection]

Above and left: Two views of *Omrah* sinking after being torpedoed on 12th May 1918.
[Both: J. and M. Clarkson collection]

Below: In August 1995, the salvage company Blue Water Recoveries discovered the wreck of *Omrah* in the Mediterranean. This UK-based company has led many successful salvage operations including the 2002 expedition to find HMS *Hood*. This shows the spirket plate at the top of *Omrah's* bow.
[Both: Blue Water Recoveries Ltd.]

ORTONA 1899-1906 Twin screw
O.N. 110613 7,945g 4,115n 500 x 55.3 x 33.7 feet.
1910: 8,939g 4,934n
Two T.3-cyl by Vickers Sons and Maxim Ltd., Barrow-in-Furness; 1,750 NHP, 10,000 IHP, 18 knots.
Passengers: 140 first, 180 second, 300 third.
Refrigerated space: 58,349 cubic feet.
10.7.1899: Launched by Vickers Sons and Maxim Ltd., Barrow-in-Furness (Yard No. 272).
26.10.1899: Registered at Liverpool in the ownership of the Pacific Steam Navigation Company, Liverpool as ORTONA.
24.11.1899: Left on maiden voyage from London to Australia.
7.9.1902-31.12.1902: Boer War Transport No. 12.
8.5.1906: Sold to Royal Mail Steam Packet Company, London.

15.5.1906: Registered at London.
30.4.1909: Left on final voyage from London to Australia for the Orient-Royal Mail Steam Packet Company joint service.
1910: Sent to Harland and Wolff Ltd., Belfast for conversion into a 320-passenger capacity cruise ship.
21.9.1910: Renamed ARCADIAN.
23.9.1911: Registered at Belfast.
1.1912: First cruise as the world's largest full-time cruise ship.
15.4.1917: Torpedoed and sunk by the German submarine UC 74 near Milo Island, Greece in position 36.50 north by 24.50 east whilst on a voyage from Salonica to Alexandria with troops. 277 lives were lost.
8.6.1917: Register closed.

Ortona (above) and as *Arcadian* (below).   *[Both: Peter Newall collection]*

ORONTES (1) 1902-1922 Twin screw
O.N. 115707 9,023g 4,622n 513.7 x 58.2 x 34.5 feet.
Two Q.4-cyl. by Fairfield Shipbuilding and Engineering Co. Ltd.,
Glasgow; 1,700 NHP, 10,000 IHP, 18 knots.
Passengers: 152 first, 147 second, 368 third.
Refrigerated space: 69,533 cubic feet.
10.5.1902: Launched by Fairfield Shipbuilding and Engineering Co.
Ltd., Glasgow (Yard No. 418).
10.9.1902: Registered at Glasgow in the ownership of the Orient
Steam Navigation Co. Ltd., London as ORONTES.
24.10.1902: Left on maiden voyage from London to Australia.
11.1915-8.1916: Chartered as freight and troop transport.
10.1916: Became full-time troop transport.

10.1916-8.1917: Requisitioned under Liner Requisition Scheme as
a troop transport.
6.17.1921: Laid up off Southend.
25.1.1923: Sold to British World Trade Expeditions Ltd., London
for use a floating exhibition ship. This was the second attempt at a
deal as the first on 16.2.1922 was never completed.
27.1.1923: Registered at London. Was to be renamed BRITISH
TRADE and converted at Hull but venture failed and company went
into receivership
1924: Laid up off Southend.
1925: Sold by liquidators to T.W. Ward Ltd., Sheffield for scrap.
2.11.1925: Demolition commenced at Inverkeithing.
4.2.1926: Register closed.

The brand-new *Orontes* (1) on the Clyde (above) and post 1906 with a yellow funnel, opposite the Tilbury Hotel, River Thames (below).
[Above: Glasgow University Archives DC101/0465; below: Peter Newall collection]

SHIPS OF THE ORIENT STEAM NAVIGATION CO. LTD.
1909-1966
All are steel vessels

Orsova (1), the first of five new liners delivered in 1909, on trials (above) and at the Tilbury Landing Stage in the 1930s with a Gravesend-Tilbury ferry in the foreground (below left).

[Above: Glasgow University Archives DC101.0469; below left: Peter Newall collection]

ORSOVA (1) 1909-1936 Twin screw
O.N. 128278 12,036g 6,831n 536.2 x 63.3 x 34.3 feet.
Two Q.4-cyl. by John Brown and Co. Ltd., Clydebank; 1,987 NHP, 14,000 IHP, 18 knots.
Passengers: 287 first, 126 second, 660 third (1933: 660 tourist).
Refrigerated space: 88,250 cubic feet.
7.11.1908: Launched by John Brown and Co. Ltd., Clydebank (Yard No. 383).
24.5.1909: Registered at Glasgow in the ownership of the Orient Steam Navigation Co. Ltd., London as ORSOVA.
25.6.1909: Sailed on maiden voyage from London to Australia.
4.1915: Chartered as a troop transport.
14.3.1917: Seriously damaged by a mine laid by the German submarine UC 68 near the Eddystone and beached in Cawsand Bay. Eight lives were lost.
17.3.1917: Refloated and taken to Devonport for repairs.
9.1918: Returned to service.
10.1918-5.1919: Requisitioned under the Liner Requisition Scheme as a troop transport.
1933: Converted to tourist class only ship.
9.1936: Sold for scrap.
21.10.1936: Arrived Bo'ness for demolition by P. and W. MacLellan Ltd.
13.2.1937: Register closed.

OTWAY 1909-1917 Twin screw
O.N. 128282 12,077g 6,690n 535.9 x 63.2 x 34.2 feet.
Two Q.4-cyl. by Fairfield Shipbuilding and Engineering Co. Ltd., Glasgow; 2,000 NHP, 14,000 IHP, 10,000 SHP, 18 knots.
Passengers: 280 first, 115 second, 700 third.
Refrigerated space: 91,000 cubic feet.
21.11.1908: Launched by Fairfield Shipbuilding and Engineering Co. Ltd., Govan (Yard No. 459).
25.5.1909: Registered at Glasgow in the ownership of the Orient Steam Navigation Co. Ltd., London as OTWAY.
9.7.1909: Sailed on maiden voyage from London to Australia.
11.11.1914: Requisitioned by Admiralty for use as an armed merchant cruiser in the Tenth Cruiser Squadron.
23.11.1914: Commissioned as HMS OTWAY.
23.7.1917: Torpedoed by German submarine UC 49 north of the Butt of Lewis in position 58.54 north by 06.28 west. Ten lives were lost.
3.9.1917: Register closed.

Otway on trials (above) and in Australian waters (below).
[Above: Glasgow University Archives DC101/0470 (09); below: Ian Farquhar collection]

Osterley photographed in the Thames by F.C. Gould (top); in drydock at Cockatoo Island, Sydney (middle) and at Cape Town in 1919 or 1920 with much activity in the foreground (bottom).

[Top: The Ballast Trust; middle: Ambrose Greenway collection; bottom: Ship Society of South Africa/Martin Leendertz collection]

OSTERLEY 1909-1930 Twin screw
O.N. 128287 12,129g 6,781n 535.0 x 63.2 x 34.1 feet.
Two Q.4-cyl. by London and Glasgow Engineering and Shipbuilding Co. Ltd., Govan; 1,973 NHP, 14,000 IHP, 18 knots.
Passengers: 282 first, 130 second, 688 third.
Refrigerated space: 92,940 cubic feet.
26.1.1909: Launched by London and Glasgow Engineering and Shipbuilding Co. Ltd., Govan (Yard No. 333). Original launch planned for *21.1* but stuck 40 feet down the ways after frost hardened the tallow.
16.6.1909: Registered at Glasgow in the ownership of the Orient Steam Navigation Co. Ltd., London as OSTERLEY.
6.8.1909: Sailed on maiden voyage from London to Australia.
5.11.1909: Badly damaged at Port Said in collision with Russian steamer ROMAN (2,413/1890 ex OVINGDEAN GRANGE). Returned to builders for three weeks repairs.
4.1917-5.1919: Requisitioned under Liner Requisition Scheme as a troop transport.
3.1930: Sold for scrap to P. and W. MacLellan, Glasgow.
14.4.1930: Arrived Bo'ness for demolition.
25.4.1930: Register closed.

The dazzle-painted *Osterley* at New York on Peace Day 1918 (top) and her gun crew in July 1915 (left).
[Top: Sydney Maritime Museum Ltd; left J. and M. Clarkson collection]

Coaling *Osterley* at an unknown port.
[J. and M. Clarkson collection]

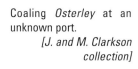

OTRANTO (1) 1909-1918 Twin screw

O.N. 124675 12,124g 7,433n 535.3 x 64.0 x 38.6 feet.
Two Q.4-cyl. by Workman, Clark and Co. Ltd., Belfast; 1,976 NHP, 14,000 IHP, 18 knots.
Passengers: 235 first, 186 second, 696 third.
Refrigerated space: 95,000 cubic feet.
27.3.1909: Launched by Workman, Clark and Co. Ltd., Belfast (Yard No. 278).
20.7.1909: Registered at Belfast in the ownership of the Orient Steam Navigation Co. Ltd., London as OTRANTO.

1.10.1909: Sailed on maiden voyage from London to Australia.
4.8.1914: Requisitioned by the Admiralty for use as an armed merchant cruiser.
11.8.1914: Commissioned as HMS OTRANTO.
6.10.1918: Drifted ashore on Islay, Scotland, in bad weather after being hit amidships by the P&O steamer KASHMIR (8,841/1915) whilst in a convoy from New York to Liverpool. 431 lives were lost, mainly United States troops.
3.9.1920: Register closed.

The two Belfast-built ships, *Otranto* (1) and *Orvieto,* did not have the superstructure extending to the foremast.
Above: *Otranto* (1) at Hobart. *[Ian Farquhar collection].*
Below: As an armed merchant cruiser, *HMS Otranto* sank with great loss of life in 1918. *[Imperial War Museum SP1064]*

ORVIETO 1909-1931 Twin screw
O.N. 129628 12,130g 7,421n 535.3 x 64.0 x 38.6 feet
Two Q.4-cyl. by Workman, Clark and Co. Ltd., Belfast; 1,976 NHP, 14,000 IHP, 18 knots.
Passengers: 235 first, 186 second, 696 third.
Refrigerated space: 95,000 cubic feet.
6.7.1909: Launched by Workman, Clark and Co. Ltd., Belfast (Yard No. 279).
4.11.1909: Registered at Belfast in the ownership of the Orient Steam Navigation Co. Ltd., London as ORVIETO.

26.11.1909: Sailed on maiden voyage from London to Australia.
11.1914: Used as a troop transport between Sydney and Egypt.
3.1915: Requisitioned by the Admiralty for use as an armed minelayer.
8.3.1915: Commissioned as HMS ORVIETO.
26.5.1916-19.10.1919: Requisitioned as an armed merchant cruiser in the Tenth Cruiser Squadron.
30.3.1931: Sold to P. and W. MacLellan Ltd., Glasgow.
3.4.1931: Arrived at Bo'ness for demolition.
17.4.1931: Register closed.

Orvieto on trials (above) and in Australian waters (below). *[Above: Ambrose Greenway collection; below: J. and M. Clarkson collection]*

Orama (1) off Gravesend in January 1914 (top) and as the armed merchant cruiser *HMS Orama* (middle).
HMS Orama's guns (bottom) sank Hamburg-Amerika Linie's *Navarra* (5,794/1906) off the River Plate on 11th November 1914.
[Top and bottom: National Maritime Museum G.102 and N.46050; middle J. and M. Clarkson collection]

ORAMA (1) 1911-1917 Triple screw
O.N. 132989 12,927g 8,179n 551.0 x 64.2 x 39 feet.
Two T.4-cyl. plus low-pressure turbine by John Brown and Co. Ltd.,
Clydebank; 1,976 NHP, 14,000 IHP, 18 knots.
Passengers: 240 first, 210 second, 630 third.
Refrigerated space: 97,817 cubic feet.
28.6.1911: Launched by John Brown and Co. Ltd., Clydebank
(Yard No. 403).
7.11.1911: Registered at Glasgow in the ownership of the Orient
Steam Navigation Co. Ltd., London as ORAMA.
10.11.1911: Sailed on maiden voyage from London to Australia.
4.9.1914: Requisitioned by the Admiralty as an armed merchant
cruiser.
12.9.1914: Commissioned as HMS ORAMA.
19.10.1917: Torpedoed and sunk by the German submarine U 62 in
the North Atlantic in position 48.00 north by 09.20 west.
16.11.1917: Register closed.

ORMONDE 1917-1952 Twin screw
O.N. 141866 14,852g 9,021n 580.5 x 66.7 x 40.5 feet.
Six Brown-Curtis geared steam turbines by John Brown and Co.
Ltd., Clydebank; 2,120 NHP, 15,000 SHP, 18 knots.
Passengers: 278 first, 196 second, 1,017 third (*1933*: 779 tourist
1949: 1,052 tourist).
Refrigerated space: 101,635 cubic feet.
21.10.1913: Keel laid.
10.2.1917: Launched by John Brown and Co. Ltd., Clydebank (Yard
No. 425).
10.1917: Requisitioned under Liner Requisition Scheme as a troop
transport.
5.12.1917: Registered at Glasgow in the ownership of the Orient
Steam Navigation Co. Ltd., London as ORMONDE.
15.11.1919: Sailed on first voyage from London to Australia.

1923: Converted to oil firing.
1933: Converted to a tourist-class only ship.
29.11.1939: Requisitioned as a troop transport.
31.3.1947: Sent for reconditioning by Cammell Laird and Co. Ltd.,
Birkenhead.
34.9.1947: Handed back to owners.
10.10.1947: Sailed on first post-war voyage from London to
Australia as a one-class emigrant ship.
1952: Sold to British Iron and Steel Corporation (BISCO).
5.12.1952: Delivered to W.H. Arnott, Young and Co. at Dalmuir for
partial demolition.
25.5.1953: Towed to Troon for demolition to be completed by the
West of Scotland Shipbreaking Co. Ltd.
18.10.1954: Register closed.

Ormonde in peacetime colours (above) and at Sydney in First World War camouflage whilst serving as a troop transport (below).
[Above: J. and M. Clarkson collection; below: Ian Farquhar collection]

85

Königin Luise was one of eight similar ships built for Norddeutscher Lloyd between 1896 and 1900.
[*Ian Farquhar collection*]

Omar. [Ian Farquhar collection]

OMAR 1920-1924 Twin screw
O.N. 143196 10,711g 6,790n 523.1 x 60.1 x 34.9 feet.
Two Q.4-cyl. by A.G. Vulcan, Stettin; 846 NHP, 6,000 IHP, 13.5 knots.
Passengers: 225 first, 235 second, 1,940 third (Orient Line service: 70 first, 757 third).
17.10.1896: Launched by A.G. Vulcan, Stettin (Yard No. 232).
16.3.1897: Completed for Norddeutscher Lloyd, Bremen, Germany as KÖNIGIN LUISE.
22.3.1897: Sailed on maiden voyage from Bremerhaven to New York.
10.4.1919: Handed over to Great Britain as a war reparation.
8.5.1919: Registered in the ownership of the Shipping Controller (Orient Steam Navigation Co. Ltd., managers), London.
20.8.1920: Acquired by the Orient Steam Navigation Co. Ltd., London.
4.9.1920: Sailed on first voyage from London to Australia.
8.9.1920: Collided with the steamer LOUGHBOROUGH (3,073/1905) in fog off Lisbon.
2.11.1920: Renamed OMAR.
4.7.1924: Sold to Byron Steam Ship Co. Ltd., London and renamed EDISON for use on a Piraeus to New York passenger service.
1929: Registered at Piraeus in the ownership of the National Steam Navigation Co. of Greece.
10.7.1929: UK register closed.
30.7.1935: Arrived at Genoa for demolition.

Omar. [The Ballast Trust]

ORCADES (1) 1921-1925 Twin screw

O.N. 143122 9,630g 5,704n 492.0 x 57.6 x 35 feet.
Two Q.4-cyl. by A.G. Vulkan, Stettin; 836 NHP, 7,000 IHP, 15 knots.
Passengers: 148 first, 162 second, 453 third (Orient Line service: 123 first, 476 third).
12.5.1906: Launched by A.G. Vulkan, Stettin (Yard No. 265).
9.8.1906: Completed for Norddeutscher Lloyd, Bremen, Germany as PRINZ LUDWIG.
16.8.1906: Sailed on maiden voyage from Bremerhaven to the Far East.
27.3.1919: Handed over to Great Britain as war reparation.

14.4.1919: Registered in the ownership of the Shipping Controller (P&O Steam Navigation Company, managers), London.
10.3.1921: Acquired by the Orient Steam Navigation Co. Ltd., London.
29.9.21: Renamed ORCADES.
7.10.1921: Registered at London.
8.10.1921: Sailed on first voyage from London to Australia.
30.3.1925: Register closed on sale to M. Stern A.G., Bremerhaven, Germany.
2.4.1925: Left London in tow for Bremerhaven.
1926: Broken up in third quarter.

Prinz Ludwig was a modified, two-funnelled version of the thirteen-ship *Feldherren*-class of NDL passenger-cargo vessels. *[Arnold Kludas collection]*

Orcades (1) in Sydney. *[Ian Farquhar collection]*

Although built for Norddeutscher Lloyd, *Zeppelin* only saw NDL service in 1927 as *Dresden.* As *Ormuz* she was the largest of Orient Line's ex-German liners. As *Dresden* she was wrecked at Karmøysund during a Norwegian cruise in 1934.
Above: *Ormuz* (2) in the Thames. *[Peter Newall collection]*   Below: *Dresden. [Prof. Theodor F. Siersdorfer]*

ORMUZ (2)   1921-1927   Twin screw steamer
O.N. 144399   14,588g 8,082n 550.0 x 67.2 x 35.1 feet
Two Q.4-cyl. by Bremer Vulkan, Vegesack; 1,100 NHP, 9,600 IHP, 15.5 knots.
Passengers: 156 first, 342 second, 1,348 third (Orient Line service: 308 first, 880 third).
Refrigerated space: 99,710 cubic feet.
9.6.1914: Launched by Bremer Vulkan, Vegesack (Yard No. 579).
21.1.1915: Completed for Norddeutscher Lloyd, Bremen, Germany as ZEPPELIN. Laid up during the First World War.
28.3.1919: Delivered to Allies as a war reparation. Used initially as a United States transport before being handed over to Great Britain.
11.9.1919: Registered in the ownership of the Shipping Controller (White Star Line, managers), London.
10.12.1920: Renamed ORMUZ (her name had been announced as ORFORD).
28.3.1921: Acquired by Orient Steam Navigation Co. Ltd., London.
14.6.1921: Registered at London.
12.11.1921: Sailed on first voyage from London to Australia.
4.1927: Sold to Norddeutscher Lloyd, Bremen, Germany and renamed DRESDEN.
21.4.1927: UK register closed.
20.6.1934: Struck rock at Klepp Bokn Island, Karmøysund, Norway and beached near Blikshavn whilst on a cruise from Bremerhaven. Three lives were lost.
21.6.1934: Sank. Wreck later sold for scrap to a company in Stavanger.

Dresden in service and two views of her wreck. *[Top: G.R. Scott collection; middle: Prof. Theodor F. Siersdorfer; bottom: J. and M. Clarkson collection]*

Top: *Orama* (2) was the first of the new 20,000-tonners built in the 1920s.   *[Ian Farquhar collection]*
Right: *Orama* (2) at Tilbury with the experimental corn-coloured hull.
               [R.A.F. Museum, Charles E. Brown collection 5445-4]

ORAMA (2) 1924-1940 Twin screw
O.N. 146024 19,770g 11,942n 632.0 x 75.2 x 32.9 feet.
Six Parsons-type geared steam turbines by Vickers Ltd., Barrow-in-Furness; 3,856 NHP, 20,000 SHP, 20 knots.
Passengers: 592 first, 1,192 third (1935: 484 first, 498 tourist)
Refrigerated space: 187,325 cubic feet
20.5.1924: Launched by Vickers Ltd., Barrow-in-Furness (Yard No. 598).
9.10.1924: Registered at Barrow-in-Furness in the ownership of the Orient Steam Navigation Co. Ltd., London as ORAMA.
15.11.1924: Sailed on first voyage from London to Australia.
10.1934: Hull painted corn colour as trial prior to arrival of ORION.
8.12.1939: Requisitioned as a troop transport.
8.6.1940: Attacked by gunfire from the German heavy cruiser ADMIRAL HIPPER and destroyer HANS LODY in the North Sea in position 67.44 north by 3.52 east whilst on a voyage from Scapa Flow to Narvik in ballast. The latter sank her with two torpedoes. Twenty members of the crew were killed and the remainder were rescued by the Germans and sent to prisoner-of-war camps.
9.11.1940: Register closed.

On her way to assist in the evacuation of troops from Narvik, *Orama* (2) was intercepted by the German warships *Admiral Hipper* and *Hans Lody*. The two German ships pounded her with their guns. As she started to list, the crew took to the lifeboats on the starboard side. *Orama* was then torpedoed by *Hans Lody*. This series of photographs, starting opposite page bottom left, follow through from the attack to her demise along with the two warships involved. Note what appears to be a shell hole in the afterside of the forward funnel. *[All: WB-Bilddienst]*

ORONSAY (1) 1925-1942 Twin screw
O.N. 147948 20,001g 11,441n 633.6 x 75.2 x 33.0 feet.
Six Brown-Curtis geared steam turbines by John Brown and Co. Ltd., Clydebank; 3,811 NHP, 20,000 SHP, 20 knots.
Passengers: 596 first, 1,184 third (*1935:* 501 first, 482 tourist).
Refrigerated space: 163,570 cubic feet.
14.8.1924: Launched by John Brown and Co. Ltd., Clydebank (Yard No. 500).
30.1.1925: Registered at Glasgow in the ownership of the Orient Steam Navigation Co. Ltd., London as ORONSAY.
7.2.1925: Sailed on maiden voyage from London to Australia.

24.12.1932: Inaugurated the first cruise from Australia for Orient Line.
6.4.1940: Requisitioned as a troop transport.
17.6.1940: Damaged at St. Nazaire during an air raid.
9.10.1942: Torpedoed and sunk by the Italian submarine ARCHIMEDE off West Africa in position 04.29 north by 20.52 west whilst on a voyage from Cape Town to the UK via Freetown with passengers and a cargo of copper and oranges. Six members of the crew were lost.
7.1.1943: Register closed.

The first Orient liner over 20,000 tons, *Oronsay* (1) was also the only post-war new-build not to come from Barrow-in-Furness.
[Above: Ian Farquahar collection; below: Peter Newall collection]

92

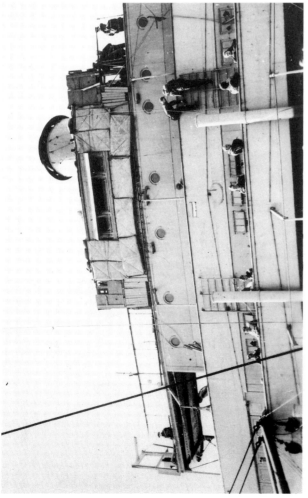

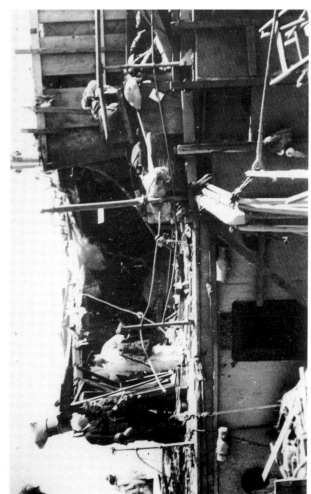

During the evacuation of British troops from St. Nazaire, *Oronsay* (1) sustained considerable damage in an air raid, including the destruction of her chartroom. In the same attack Cunard Line's *Lancastria* (16,243/1922) suffered a direct hit and more than 3,000 died in one of the worst maritime disasters of the war. Many of the survivors were rescued by *Oronsay* (1). *[Imperial War Museum]*

OTRANTO (2) 1926-1957 Twin screw

O.N. 146025 20,032g 12,031n 632.0 x 75.2 x 32.9 feet.
Six Parsons-type geared steam turbines by Vickers Ltd., Barrow-in-Furness; 3,722 NHP, 20,000 SHP, 20 knots.
Passengers: 572 first, 1,168 third (*1935:* 512 first, 476 tourist; *1949:* 1,412 tourist.
Refrigerated space: 170,688 cubic feet.
9.6.1925: Launched by Vickers Ltd., Barrow-in-Furness (Yard No. 619).
12.1925: Registered at Barrow-in-Furness in the ownership of the Orient Steam Navigation Co. Ltd., London as OTRANTO.
9.1.1926: Sailed on maiden voyage from London to Australia.
11.5.1926: Severely damaged bow striking cliffs near Cape Grosso, Greece. She was later repaired at Southampton.
11.8.1928: Damaged bow in collision with the Japanese steamer

KITANO MARU (7,951/1919) when beginning a cruise from Immingham to the North Cape.
25.11.1939: Requisitioned as a troop transport.
11.1942: Converted into a Large Assault Ship and fitted with assault landing craft. Took part in the North African landings during Operation Torch, the invasion of Sicily and the landings at Salerno before reverting to troopship duty.
10.5.1948: Sent to Cammell Laird and Co. Ltd., Birkenhead for reconditioning prior to being handed back to owners.
14.7.1949: Sailed on first post-war London to Australia voyage as a one-class emigrant ship.
4.1957: Sold to British Iron and Steel Corporation (BISCO).
14.6.1957: Arrived at Faslane for demolition by Shipbreaking Industries Ltd.

Above: *Otranto* (2) was in Orient Line service for thirty-one years. *[The Ballast Trust]*
Below: *Otranto* (2) in Cape Town during her final Australian voyage in 1957. She sailed round the Cape because of the closure of the Suez Canal. *[George Aschman]*

Between 1926 and 1928 *Otranto* (2) twice damaged her bow in collisions. The first incident happened when she hit cliffs at Cape Grosso near Cape Matapan, Greece whilst on a cruise which included a visit to the battlefields of Gallipoli with relatives of the fallen soldiers. This series of photos taken in Greece shows the extent of the damage and the Swedish salvage vessel *Hermes* (430/1888).

[All: J. and M. Clarkson collection]

Otranto (2) was fitted with assault landing craft for the North African invasion and landings in Italy. Here are two views of her as a troopship, her landing craft clearly visible in the lower photograph.
[Above: National Maritime Museum N.36322; below: Imperial War Museum FL12791]

ORFORD 1928-1940 Twin screw

O.N. 146026 19,941g 12,027n 632.2 x 75.4 x 33.1 feet.

Six Parsons-type geared steam turbines by Vickers Ltd., Barrow-in-Furness; 3,825 NHP, 20,000 SHP, 20 knots.

Passengers: 520 first, 1,162 third (*1935:* 468 first, 518 tourist).

27.9.1927: Launched by Vickers Ltd., Barrow-in-Furness (Yard No. 627).

24.2.1928: Registered at Barrow-in-Furness in the ownership of the Orient Steam Navigation Co. Ltd., London as ORFORD.

13.10.1928: Sailed on maiden voyage from London to Australia.

26.8.1939: Requisitioned as a troop transport.

1.10.1939: Requisition ended.

20.11.1939: Requisitioned again as a troop transport.

1.6.1940: Bombed by German aircraft at Marseilles and beached whilst on a voyage from Marseilles to Mombasa. Fourteen lives were lost.

2.12.1940: Register closed.

4.9.1941: After salvage and sale to shipbreakers at La Seyne, left Marseilles under tow. By 1944 the hull had been demolished almost down to the waterline.

31.7.1947: Arrived at Savona for demolition to be completed.

Orford at Melbourne (top), in the Thames 26th October 1935 (middle) and during a Norwegian cruise in the 1930s (bottom).

[Top: Ian Farquhar collection; middle and bottom: Peter Newall collection]

Orontes (2) was the last of the Barrow-built two funnelled ships and the only one to have a raked bow. *[Peter Newall collection]*

ORONTES (2) 1929-1962 Twin screw

O.N. 146027 19,970g 12,010n 638.2 x 75.3 x 33.1 feet.
Six Parsons-type geared steam turbines by Vickers-Armstrongs Ltd., Barrow-in-Furness; 3,825 NHP, 20,000 SHP, 20 knots.
Passengers: 508 first, 1,112 third (*1935:* 463 first, 528 tourist *1948:* 502 first, 618 tourist; *1953:* 1,410 tourist).
26.2.1929: Launched by Vickers-Armstrongs Ltd., Barrow-in-Furness (Yard No. 637).
9.1929: Registered at Barrow-in-Furness in the ownership of the Orient Steam Navigation Co. Ltd., London as ORONTES.
26.10.1929: Sailed on maiden voyage from London to Australia.
4.1.1940: Requisitioned as a troop transport.
1.3.1947: Sent for reconditioning by John I. Thornycroft and Co., Southampton.
14.5.1948: Handed back to owners.
17.6.1948: Left on first post-war voyage from London to Australia.
1953: Became a one-class ship.
2.1962: Sold to J.F. Ordaz y Compania, Madrid, Spain for scrap.
5.3.1962: Arrived at Valencia.

Above left: *Orontes* (2) probably at Tilbury. *[World Ship Photo Library]*
Above right: Towards the end of her post-war refit and still painted grey, *Orontes* (2) at Southampton in March 1948.
[World Ship Photo Library]

Orontes (2) at Aden. *[Ambrose Greenway collection]*

The brand-new *Orion* in the Mersey in July 1935 photographed by Basil Feilden (top and middle). Because of problems with soot on deck, her funnel was later raised by nine feet, as seen in this classic Cape Town view taken in June 1961 (bottom), a change which was also incorporated on *Orcades* (2).

[Top and middle: J. and M. Clarkson; bottom: Robert Pabst]

ORION 1935-1963 Twin screw

O.N. 164493 23,371g 14,032n 640.3 x 82.2 x 33.7 feet
Six Parsons-type geared steam turbines by Vickers-Armstrongs Ltd., Barrow-in-Furness; 4,912 NHP, 24,000 SHP, 20 knots.
Passengers: 484 first, 637 tourist (*1947:* 550 first, 700 tourist *1958:* 342 cabin, 722 tourist; *1961:* 1,691 tourist.
Refrigerated space: 209,215 cubic feet.
7.12.1934: Launched by Vickers-Armstrongs Ltd., Barrow-in-Furness (Yard No. 697).
7.1935: Completed for Orient Steam Navigation Co. Ltd., London as ORION.
28.9.1935: Sailed on maiden voyage from London to Australia.
21.8-12.9.1936: Guarantee dry-docking at Southampton which probably including heightening of funnel by nine feet.
26.8.1939: Requisitioned and converted at Sydney to a troop transport.
30.9.1939: Released from requisition.
2.12.1939: Requisitioned again as a troop transport.

2.9.1942: Collided with stern of HMS REVENGE during convoy to Suez via Cape Town, in position 10.36 south by 04.12 west. Bow badly damaged. Temporary repairs made at Cape Town with full repairs at Singapore during November/December.
18.4.1946: Released from service.
1.5.1946: Sent to be reconditioned by Vickers-Armstrongs Ltd., Barrow-in-Furness.
25.1.1947: Handed back to owners.
25.2.1947: Sailed on first post-war voyage from London to Australia.
1960: Transferred to P&O-Orient Lines.
23.5-30.9.1963: Chartered to Firma Otto Friederich Behnke as a hotel-ship for visitors to the 1963 Hamburg International Horticultural Exhibition.
7.10.1963: Arrived at Antwerp for demolition at Tamise by Jos. Boel et fils, S.A., Belgium.
30.11.1963: Work commenced.

Orion in the large dry dock at Tilbury on 17th March 1954. *[Aerofilms Ltd. A.53229]*

ORCADES (2) 1937-1942 Twin screw
O.N. 165501 23,456g 14,029n 639.3 x 82.2 x 33.6 feet
Six Parsons-type geared steam turbines by Vickers-Armstrongs Ltd., Barrow-in-Furness; 4,912 NHP, 24,000 SHP, 20 knots.
Passengers: 463 first, 605 tourist.
Refrigerated space: 208,190 cubic feet.
1.12.1936: Launched by Vickers-Armstrongs Ltd., Barrow-in-Furness (Yard No. 712).
2.7.1937: Registered at London in the ownership of the Orient Steam Navigation Co. Ltd., London as ORCADES.
9.10.1937: Sailed on maiden voyage from London to Australia.

18.5.1939: Returned to Barrow for refit following engine trouble.
28.8.1939: Requisitioned as a troop transport.
17.10.1939: Released from requisition.
27.11.1939: Requisitioned again as troop transport.
10.10.1942: Torpedoed and sunk by the German submarine U 172 in the South Atlantic, 280 miles north west of Cape Town, in position 35.51 south by 14.40 east whilst on a voyage from Cape Town to the UK with passengers and general cargo. Forty-six lives were lost.
6.1.1943: Register closed.

As well as a taller funnel, *Orcades* (2) had cleaner lines than *Orion* with wider spaced and thicker, arched stanchions. This difference can be clearly seen in the photograph below showing *Orcades* (2) as a troopship with a black hull leaving Lyttelton on 27th August 1940 with New Zealand troops bound for the Middle East. *[Ballast Trust; Ian Farquhar collection]*

In March 1941 *Orcades* (2) joined the largest ever convoy to leave the shores of Britain to that date and is seen here in the Clyde. Twenty-three troopships took part including four Orient liners. When the convoy reached Cape Town on 18th April, a famous panoramic photo of the Victoria Basin and the Duncan Dock was taken by a local photographer, John Marsh, from the top of the grain elevator. Below is a section of the picture showing the Victoria Basin with *Orcades* (2) alongside the grain hoppers of Collier Jetty and on the left the Norwegian tanker *Dageid;* King Line's *King David; Strathallan,* P&O's 'sister' to *Orcades* (2); Royal Mail's *Andes;* Canadian Pacific's *Empress of Canada* on East Pier with Ellerman's *City of Melbourne* at the Elbow. To the right on the South Arm are *Orion* and her P&O 'sister' *Strathmore.*
[Top National Maritime Museum N.36213; middle and lower: John Marsh Collection, South African Maritime Museum]

103

ORCADES (3) 1948-1973 Twin screw

O.N. 182883 28,164g 15,839n 681.7 x 90.8 x 30.5 feet.
Six Parsons-type geared steam turbines by Vickers-Armstrongs Ltd., Barrow-in-Furness; 42,500 SHP, 22.5 knots.
Passengers: 773 first, 772 tourist (*1959:* 631 first, 734 tourist; *1964:* 1,635 tourist).
Refrigerated space: 238,460 cubic feet.
14.10.1947: Launched by Vickers-Armstrongs Ltd., Barrow-in-Furness (Yard No. 950).
11.1948: Registered at London in the ownership of the Orient Steam Navigation Co. Ltd., London as ORCADES.
14.12.1948: Sailed on maiden voyage from London to Australia.

Reduced pre-war Orient Line schedule to Australia by ten days.
1954: Fitted with 'Welsh Hat' on funnel to reduce soot on deck.
1.1959: Refit at Harland and Wolff Ltd., Belfast which included air-conditioning throughout the ship - the first Orient liner with this feature.
2.5.1960: Transferred to P&O-Orient Lines.
21.9.1962: Registered ownership transferred to Peninsular and Oriental Steam Navigation Company.
6.2.1973: Arrived at Kaohsiung for demolition by Nan Feng Steel Enterprise Co. Ltd., Taiwan.
15.3.1973: Work commenced.

Given the name of the liner lost during the war, *Orcades* (3) was the first of the post-Second World War ships. She is seen in the English Channel (opposite), on trials in 1948 (above) and in the Suez Canal (below). She was fitted with a 'Welsh hat' in 1954 to reduce the amount of soot on deck. *[Opposite: Fotoflite incorporating Skyfotos; above: Peter Newall collection; below: Ambrose Greenway collection]*

ORONSAY (2) 1951-1975 Twin screw

O.N. 184415 27,632g 15,122n 681.7 x 90.1 x 30.5 feet
Six Pametrada-type geared steam turbines by Vickers-Armstrongs Ltd., Barrow-in-Furness; 42,500 SHP, 22.5 knots.
Passengers: 668 first, 833 tourist; 1972 1,400 tourist.
Refrigerated space: 222,990 cubic feet.
30.6.1950: Launched by Vickers-Armstrongs Ltd., Barrow-in-Furness (Yard No. 976).
28.10.1950: Damaged by fire whilst fitting out.
5.1951: Registered at London in the ownership of the Orient Steam Navigation Co. Ltd., London as ORONSAY.

16.5.1951: Sailed on maiden voyage from London to Australia.
1954: Fitted with 'Welsh Hat' on funnel to reduce soot on deck.
9-11.1959: Refit at Liverpool which included air-conditioning throughout the ship.
2.5.1960: Transferred to P&O-Orient Lines.
21.9.1962: Registered ownership transferred to Peninsular and Oriental Steam Navigation Company.
7.10.1975: Arrived at Kaohsiung for demolition by Nan Feng Steel Enterprise Co. Ltd., Taiwan.
10.4.1976: Work commenced.

Oronsay (2) in Orient Line colours as built - she too received a 'Welsh hat' in 1954.
[Above: Peter Newall collection; below: J. and M. Clarkson collection]

Two photos of *Oronsay* (2) in P&O colours with her 'Welsh hat', the lower photograph on her last sailing from Sydney.
[*Both: J. and M. Clarkson collection*]

ORSOVA (2) 1954-1974 Twin screw

O.N. 186017 28,790g 15,882n 691.0 x 90.6 x 31.0 feet.
Six Pametrada-type geared steam turbines by Vickers-Armstrongs Ltd., Barrow-in-Furness; 42,500 SHP, 22.5 knots.
Passengers: 685 first, 813 tourist.
Refrigerated space: 313,350 cubic feet.
14.5.1953: Launched by Vickers-Armstrongs Ltd., Barrow-in-Furness (Yard No. 1021).
3.1954: Registered at London in the ownership of the Orient Steam Navigation Co. Ltd., London as ORSOVA.

17.3.1954: Sailed on maiden voyage from London to Australia.
1-3.1960: Refit by Vickers-Armstrongs (Shipbuilders) Ltd., Newcastle-upon-Tyne which included air-conditioning throughout the ship.
2.5.1960: Transferred to P&O-Orient Lines.
31.3.1965: Registered ownership transferred to Peninsular and Oriental Steam Navigation Company.
14.2.1974: Arrived at Kaohsiung for demolition by Nan Feng Steel Enterprise Co. Ltd., Taiwan.
17.12.1974: Work commenced.

The handsome *Orsova* (2) had a career spanning only twenty years. On trials on the Isle of Arran measured mile with the snow-capped peak of Mullach Buidhe behind her (above) and in service (below). *[Top: The Ballast Trust]*

The bow of *Orsova* (2) had more flare than *Orcades* (3) and *Oronsay* (2). It also featured her name badge representing the Iron Gate rapids at Orsova on the Danube which was a barrier to vessels on the river. The badge was created by Lynton Lamb, designer of the exceptional glasswork on *Orion* and pre-war *Orcades* (2). All the liners from *Orion* onwards had bow badges and these opened to reveal the searchlight used during night transit of the Suez Canal. *Orion* had a badge with the knife, belt and club of the giant hunter of Greek mythology whilst the emblem for both the pre-war and post-war *Orcades* (3) was a stylised harp representing the Orcadean sagas. The badge of *Oronsay* (2) was a broadsword and circular shield belonging to the clansmen of the island of Oronsay.

In front of the bridge was an enclosed area called the Arena, which was used for deck games. With six hatches, refrigerated cargo was worked in the forward number 2 and 3 holds. *[Above: Peter Newall collection; below: Fotoflite, incorporating Skyfotos]*

GARONNE (2) 1959-1973 Tanker
O.N. 301034 24,513g 14,562n 37,383d 660.0 x 90.5 x 48.0 feet
Two Pametrada-type geared steam turbines by Vickers-Armstrongs
(Shipbuilders) Ltd., Newcastle-upon-Tyne; 17,600 SHP, 16.5 knots.
16.6.1959: Launched by Vickers-Armstrongs (Shipbuilders) Ltd.,
Newcastle-upon-Tyne (Yard No. 168).
12.1959: Registered at London in the ownership of the Orient Steam
Navigation Co. Ltd., London as GARONNE.
2.5.1960: Transferred to P&O-Orient Lines.
1963: Managers became Trident Tankers Ltd.
31.3.1965: Owners became Peninsular and Oriental Steam

Navigation Company (Trident Tankers Ltd., managers), London.
1.4.1970: Owners became Trident Tankers Ltd.
16.8.1971: Managers became P&O Bulk Shipping Division.
27.9.1972: Owners became Peninsular and Oriental Steam
Navigation Company, London.
13.4.1973: Sold to St. Thomas Maritime Co. Ltd., Monrovia,
Liberia (Karavias (London) Ltd., London) and renamed ST.
THOMAS.
1976: Sold to Union Minerals and Alloys Corporation, USA for scrap.
20.2.1976: Arrived at New York for demolition at Kearny, New
Jersey.

Opposite: The only cargo ship built for Orient Line, the tanker *Garonne* (2) was given a minute funnel. She is seen in Orient Line livery
(above) and in Trident Tanker colours (below). *[Opposite: Fotoflite incorporating Skyfotos; above: J. and M. Clarkson collection;
below: World Ship Society Photo Library]*

111

The positioning of *Oriana's* lifeboats low down in her hull, a common feature on modern cruise ships, accentuated her 'boxy' look.
[Peter Newall collection]

Oriana's stern design continued the tradition established by *Orion* and *Orcades* (2) in the 1930s - see stern view of *Orcades* (2) on page 102.
[J. and M. Clarkson collection]

ORIANA 1960-1986 Twin screw
O.N. 301235 41,915g 22,354n 740 x 97.2 x 32 feet.
Six Pametrada-type geared steam turbines by Vickers-Armstrongs Ltd., Barrow-in-Furness; 80,000 SHP, 27.5 knots.
Passengers: 685 first, 1,496 tourist; *1973:* 1,677.
Refrigerated space: 52,530 cubic feet.
3.11.1959: Launched by Vickers-Armstrongs Ltd., Barrow-in-Furness (Yard No. 1061).
15.11.1960: Delivered.
18.11.1960: Registered at London in the ownership of the Orient Steam Navigation Co. Ltd., London as ORIANA.
3.12.1960: Sailed on maiden voyage from Southampton to Australia.
3.12.1962: Damaged bow in collision with the aircraft carrier USS KEARSARGE near Long Beach, California.
1965: Owners became the Peninsular and Oriental Steam Navigation Company.

11.2.1986: Managers became P&O Lines Ltd.
30.4.1986: Sold to Daiwa House Sales Co. Ltd., Japan for use as a floating cultural attraction.
26.6.1986: Arrived at Sakai, Japan for conversion work by Hitachi Zosen.
26.6.1986: Register closed.
1987: Tourist attraction at Beppu Bay, Kyushu Island.
1995: Sold and towed to Qinhuangdao, China.
1998: Sold to Shanghai Oriana Entertainment Co. Ltd.
18.11.98: Towed to Shanghai.
28.9.2000: Sold at auction to Hangzhou Jiebaie Corporation, Shanghai.
6.2002: Towed to Dalian, China for use as a floating tourist attraction.
16.6.2004: During storm suffered damage and started to sink. Listing to port, she was stabilised by two large cranes, her fate uncertain at time of print.

The 'double E' badge of *Oriana* linked the Tudor monarch with the current Queen Elizabeth. At Aden in December 1960 on her maiden voyage. *[Peter Newall collection]*

Oriana is now a visitor attraction at Dalien, China. *[Hisashi Noma]*

LIQUID GAS AND ORE/BULK/OIL CARRIERS 1977-1987 OWNED BY ORIENT STEAM NAVIGATION CO. LTD. (P&O BULK SHIPPING DIVISION, MANAGERS)

GARINDA 1977-1984 Liquefied gas carrier
O.N. 377214 34,895g 22,916n 219.51 x 28.61 x 20.02 metres.
Six-cylinder 2SCSA oil engine by Maschinenbau Augsburg-Nürnberg, Augsburg, West Germany; 19,924 BHP, 16.75 knots.
Cargo capacity: 54,224 cubic metres.
12.6.1976: Launched by Thyssen Nordseewerke G.m.b.H., Emden, West Germany (Yard No. 459).
31.3.1977: Delivered to The Orient Steam Navigation Company Limited (P&O Bulk Shipping Division, managers), London as GARINDA.
1982: Managers became P&O Deep Sea Cargo Division.
13.12.1984: Owners became the Peninsular and Oriental Steam Navigation Company.
3.5.1985: Owners became Garinda Ltd. (P&O Ship Management

Ltd, managers), London.
3.12.1986: Sold to the Portland Co. Ltd., Hamilton, Bermuda (Rederiet Helge R. Myhre A/S, Oslo, Norway, managers).
3.1.1987: Renamed HEKABE.
1993: Managers became Kvaerner Shipping A/S, Oslo.
1995: Owners became Ocean Gas Ltd., Hamilton, Bermuda (Havtor Management A/S, Oslo).
1996: Owners became Partrederiet Bergesen d.y. Shipping D.A., Oslo (Bergesen d.y. ASA, managers) and registered at Nassau, Bahamas.
1997: Registered at Oslo, Norwegian International Register.
2000: Owners became Partrederiet Hekabe DA (Bergesen d.y. ASA, managers), Oslo, Norway.
4.2004: Still in service.

Garinda. [Fotoflite incorporating Skyfotos]

GALCONDA 1978-1985 Liquified gas carrier
O.N. 379657 34,893g 22,907n 219.51 x 28.58 x 19.99 metres.
Six-cylinder 2SCSA oil engine by Maschinenbau Augsburg-Nürnberg, Augsburg, West Germany; 19,920 BHP, 17 knots.
Cargo capacity: 54,224 cubic metres.
20.12.1977: Launched by Thyssen Nordseewerke G.m.b.H., Emden West Germany (Yard No. 461).
29.9.1978: Delivered to The Orient Steam Navigation Co. Ltd. (P&O Bulk Shipping Division, managers), London as GALCONDA.
1982: Managers became P&O Deep Sea Cargo Division.
3.5.1985: Owners became Galconda Gas Carriers Ltd.
1986: Sold to Glenwood Co. Ltd., Hamilton, Bermuda (Rederi

Helge R. Myhre A/S, Oslo, Norway, managers).
23.1.1987: Renamed HAVKONG.
1993: Managers became Kvaerner Shipping A/S, Oslo.
1995: Owners became Ocean Gas Ltd., Hamilton, Bermuda (Havtor Management A/S, Oslo).
1996: Owners became Partrederiet Bergesen d.y. Shipping D.A., Oslo (Bergesen d.y. ASA, managers) and registered at Nassau, Bahamas.
1997: Registered at Oslo, Norwegian International Register.
2000: Owners became Partrederiet Hekabe DA, Oslo (Acomarit (UK) Ltd., Glasgow, managers).
2002: Managers became V. Ships (UK) Ltd., Glasgow.
4.2004: Still in service.

Galconda. [G.R. Scott collection]

GALPARA 1978-1985 Liquified gas carrier
O.N. 377528 34,893g 22,908n 219.51 x 28.58 x 19.99 metres
Six-cylinder 2SCSA oil engine by Maschinenbau Augsburg-Nürnberg, Augsburg, West Germany; 19,920 BHP, 16.75 knots.
Cargo capacity: 54,103 cubic metres.
4.6.1977: Launched by Thyssen Nordseewerke G.m.b.H., Emden, West Germany (Yard No. 460).
31.3.1978: Delivered to The Orient Steam Navigation Co. Ltd. (P&O Bulk Shipping Division, managers), London as GALPARA.
1982: Managers became P&O Deep Sea Cargo Division.

3.5.1985: Owners became Galpara Gas Carriers Ltd.
1987: Sold to the Sayle Co. Ltd., Hamilton, Bermuda (Rederi Helge R Myhre A/S, Oslo, Norway, managers).
9.2.1987: Renamed HAVDROTT.
1993: Managers became Havtor Management A/S, Oslo.
1996: Owners became Partrederiet Bergesen d.y. Shipping D.A., Oslo (Bergesen d.y. ASA, managers) and registered at Nassau, Bahamas.
1997: Registered at Oslo, Norwegian International Register.
4.2004: Still in service.

Galpara. [G.R. Scott collection]

GARMULA 1978-1979 Liquified gas carrier

O.N. 358497 32,213g 21,515n 207.07 x 31.45 x 18.60 metres.
Seven-cylinder 2SCSA oil engine by Sulzer Brothers Ltd.,
Winterhur, Switzerland; 20,300 BHP, 17.5 knots.
Cargo capacity: 52,647 cubic metres.
28.4.1972: Launched by Moss Rosenberg Verft A/S, Stavanger,
Norway (Yard No. 195).
17.7.1972: Delivered to P&O Steam Navigation Company (P&O
Bulk Shipping Division, managers), London as GARMULA.
23.7.1978: Registered at London in the ownership of The Orient
Steam Navigation Co. Ltd. (P&O Bulk Shipping Division,
managers), London.
7.12.1979: Sold to Mundogas America Ltd., Monrovia, Liberia
(P&O Deep Sea Cargo Division, London, managers) and renamed
MUNDOGAS AMERICA.
1984: Management ceased.
1985: Owners became Mundogas Bermuda S.A., Hamilton,
Bermuda (Mundogas S.A., Panama) (Oslo Ship Management Ltd.,
Oslo, Norway, managers).

1989: Owners c/o Arbross Ltd., Hong Kong (Norwegian Ship
Management A/S., Oslo, managers).
1991: Owners c/o Enron Arbross Ship Management Co. Ltd., Hong
Kong (Norwegian Ship Management A/S., Oslo, managers).
1992: Owners became Mundogas America Ltd., Monrovia, Liberia
(Enron Arbross Ship Management Co. Ltd., Hong Kong)
(Norwegian Ship Management A/S., Oslo, managers).
1993: Owners became Gibeon Shipping (Pty.) Ltd., Monrovia
(Enron Arbross Ship Management Co. Ltd., Hong Kong)
(Norwegian Ship Management A/S., Oslo, managers).
1995: Owners c/o (Arbross Ship Management Co. Ltd., Hong Kong,
managers).
1997: Owners became Oslo Gas I.L.P (Arbross Ship Management
Co. Ltd., Hong Kong, managers), and registered in Oslo.
1998: Owners became Oslo Gas I.L.P (Arbross Ship Management
Co. Ltd., Hong Kong), (Havinvest Management A/S., Oslo,
managers) and renamed OGC AMERICA.
15.3.2002: Arrived at Alang for demolition.

Garmula. [Peter Newall collection]

GAMBHIRA 1978-1980 Liquified gas carrier

O.N. 358924 11,544g 6992n 153.22 x 21.32 x 12.35 metres.
Six-cylinder 2SCSA Sulzer oil engine by Astilleros de Cadiz S.A.,
Valencia, Spain; 9,600 BHP, 16.5 knots.
Cargo capacity: 14,101 cubic metres.
30.3.1968: Launched by Astilleros de Cadiz S.A., Seville, Spain
(Yard No.111).
4.1969: Delivered to Butano S.A., Madrid, Spain as BUTANUEVE.
1971: Sold to Arcadia Reederei G.m.b.H. & Co. Tankschiff K.G.,
Monrovia, Liberia and renamed BUTANAVAL.
20.2.1972: Acquired by Peninsular and Oriental Steam Navigation
Company (P&O Bulk Shipping Division, managers), London and
renamed GAMBHIRA.
28.3.1978: Owners became The Orient Steam Navigation Co. Ltd.
(P&O Bulk Shipping Division, managers), London.
23.7.1980: Sold to Habkarn Ltd., London and bareboat chartered
back to P&O Bulk Shipping Division.

29.9.1981: Sold to Lombard North Central Leasing Ltd., London,
charter continued.
3.5.1985: Sold to Gambhira Gas Carriers Ltd. and Gambhira (U.K.)
Ltd. (P&O Ship Management Ltd. managers), London.
3.10.1986: Sold to Bostock Co. Ltd., Hamilton, Bermuda (P&O
Ship Management Ltd., London, managers).
1988: Managers became A/S Havtor Management, Oslo, Norway.
5.1.1987: Renamed HAVPIL.
1987: Owners became Havpil Shipping Pte.Ltd. Singapore.
1991: Sold to Simba Chartering S.r.l., Acqui Terme, Italy
(Montorship Managers, Genoa, Italy, managers) and renamed
LULLIGAS.
1994: Sold to Afro Ltd., Valetta, Malta (Compagnia di Navigazione
Gas Line S.r.l., Genoa, managers) and renamed KAPITAN LUCA.
20.1.1996: Hull damaged due to ingress of water whilst near
Bangkok, Thailand. Declared a constructive total loss.
16.11.1996: Arrived at Alang for demolition.

Gambhira. [Fotoflite incorporating Skyfotos]

GARALA 1979-1985 Liquified gas carrier
O.N. 379852 34,893g 22,908n 219.51 x 28.61 x 20.02 metres.
Six-cylinder 2SCSA oil engine by Maschinenbau Augsburg-Nürnberg, Augsburg, West Germany, 19,924 BHP, 16.75 knots.
Cargo capacity: 54,224 cubic metres.
26.7.1978: Launched by Thyssen Nordseewerke G.m.b.H., Emden, West Germany (Yard No. 462).
2.5.1979: Delivered to Garala Ltd. and leased to Orient Steam Navigation Co. Ltd. (P&O Bulk Shipping Division, managers), London as GARALA.
1982: Managers became P&O Deep Sea Cargo Division.
3.5.1985: Managers became P&O Ship Management Ltd.

3.10.1986: Sold to Downing Co. Ltd., Hamilton, Bermuda (Rederiet Helge R. Myhre A/S, Oslo, Norway, managers).
24.12.1986: Renamed HEMINA.
1989: Owners became Garala Ltd., Hamilton, Bermuda.
1993: Managers became Kvaerner Shipping A/S, Oslo.
1995: Owners became Ocean Gas Ltd., Hamilton, Bermuda (Havtor Management A/S, Oslo).
1996: Owners became Partrederiet Bergesen d.y. Shipping D.A., Oslo (Bergesen d.y. ASA, managers) and registered at Nassau, Bahamas.
1999: Registered at Oslo, Norwegian International Register.
4.2004: Still in service.

Garala. [World Ship Photo Library]

MEYNELL 1977-1984 Bulk carrier
O.N. 360901 69,911g 45,000n 261.02 x 40.64 x 24.01 metres.
Eight-cylinder 2SCSA oil engine by Mitsubishi Heavy Industries
Ltd., Kobe, Japan; 22,883 BHP, 15.5 knots.
Cargo capacity: 4,926,415 cubic metres grain.
25.9.1973: Launched by Mitsubishi Heavy Industries Limited,
Hiroshima, Japan (Yard No.234).
21.12.1973: Delivered to the P&O Steam Navigation Company,
London as MEYNELL.
25.3.1977: Owners became the Orient Steam Navigation Co. Ltd.
(P&O Bulk Shipping Division, managers), London.
1982: Managers became P&O Deep Sea Cargo Division.
24.2.1983: Renamed EYNE.
6.5.1983: Renamed MEYNELL.
1983: Transferred to Moss Hutchison Line Ltd.
14.12.1983: Sold to Singapore Bulk Carriers Private Ltd. (Thome

and Co. Private Ltd., managers), Singapore and renamed TIMUR
LIGHT.
1986: Sold to Tampere Ltd. (Van Ommeren Marine (Hong Kong)
Ltd., managers), Hong Kong and renamed GLENDALE.
1987: Sold to Emblem Shipping Ltd., Panama (Fafalios Ltd.,
London) and renamed IRENE under the Greek flag.
1988: Sold to K/S Ancora (C.H. Sorensen & Sonner A/S,
managers), Arendal, Norway and renamed EL ANCORA.
1989: Owners became Bonita A/S (C.H. Sorensen & Sonner A/S,
managers), Arendal.
1992: Sold to Springbow Shipping Corporation, Monrovia, Liberia
(Polembros Shipping Ltd., London) and renamed ALINA.
12.8.1998: Arrived Gadani Beach for demolition by the Imran
Shipbreaking Company.
9.1998: Work began.

Above: *Meynell.*
[*Fotoflite incorporating Skyfotos*]

Right: *Meynell.*   [*G.R.Scott collection*]

Top opposite: *Jedforest.*
[*World Ship Photo Library*]

Lower opposite: *Kildare.*
[*World Ship Photo Library*]

JEDFOREST 1977-1987 Ore/bulk/oil carrier.
O.N. 343171 83,714g 64,441n 291.68 x 45.19 x 22.99 metres.
Eight-cylinder 2SCSA Burmeister & Wain oil engine by Eriksbergs M/V A/B, Gothenburg, Sweden; 30,400 BHP, 16.5 knots.
Cargo capacity: 6,317,747 cubic metres liquid.
25.5.1972: Delivered by Eriksbergs M/V A/B (Lindholmen Division), Gothenburg, Sweden to P&O Steam Navigation Company, London as JEDFOREST.
She had been constructed in two parts, the stern and four after holds by Eriksbergs M/V A/B (Yard No. 648), and the bow and forward six holds by Lisnave Estaleiros Navais de Lisboa S.a.r.l., Lisbon, Portugal. The two parts were joined at Gothenburg.
25.3.1977: Owners became the Orient Steam Navigation Co. Ltd.

(P&O Bulk Shipping Division, managers), London.
1982: Managers became P&O Deep Sea Cargo Division.
28.5.1986: Registered at Hong Kong.
23.2.1987: Sold to Tradeshores Line Ltd., Limassol, Cyprus (Kappa Maritime Ltd. (P.E. and G. Kollakis), London) and renamed LADY SKY.
12.4.1987: Attacked and set on fire by Iraqi aircraft when about 120 miles south of Kharg Island in position 27.45 north by 51.13 east. She was on her first loaded voyage on the Kharg Island shuttle service. Later repaired and returned to service.
1993: Sold to Stukas Shipping Co. Ltd., Cyprus, and renamed LADY STAR.
11.8.1993: Arrived Huangpu, China to be broken up.

KILDARE 1977-1987 Ore/bulk/oil carrier
O.N. 358610 83,714g 64,441n 291.65 x 45.19 x 23.02 metres.
Eight-cylinder 2SCSA Burmeister & Wain-type oil engine by Eriksbergs M/V A/B, Gothenburg, Sweden; 30,400 BHP, 16.25 knots.
Cargo capacity: 4,926,442 cubic metres grain.
7.7.1972: Launched by Eriksbergs M/V A/B (Lindholmen Division), Gothenburg, Sweden. (Yard No. 649).
10.1972: Delivered to the P&O Steam Navigation Company (P&O Bulk Shipping Division, managers), London as KILDARE.
4.1.1978: Transferred to the Orient Steam Navigation Co. Ltd. (P&O Bulk Shipping Division, managers), London.

1982: Managers became P&O Deep Sea Cargo Division.
20.4.1986: Registered at Hong Kong.
27.2.1987: Sold to Globewind Ltd (P&O Ship Management (Hong Kong) Ltd., managers), Hong Kong and chartered back.
1989: Managers became Sealuck Shipping Co (Pte.) Ltd., Singapore and renamed NEW PHASE.
1990: Sold to Sycamore Shipping Ltd., Monrovia, Liberia (Société Anonyme Monegasque D'Administration Maritime et Aerienne, Monte Carlo) and renamed SILVER CLOUD under the Panama flag.
21.1.1993: Arrived in mainland China to be broken up.

IRFON 1978-1985 Ore/bulk/oil carrier
O.N. 341450 82,206g 61,481n 288.50 x 43.49 x 23.70 metres.
Two steam turbines manufactured by A.E.G. West Berlin, West
Germany, double reduction geared to a single screw shaft; 24,000
SHP, 15.75 knots.
Cargo capacity: 5,977,558 cubic metres grain, 5,966,363 cubic
metres liquid.
15.6.1971: Launched by Howaldtswerke-Deutsche Werft, Kiel,
West Germany (Yard No.11).
5.11.1971: Delivered to the P&O Steam Navigation Company

(P&O Bulk Shipping Division, managers), London. Her intended
name was ISLE OF WIGHT.
4.1.1978: Owners became The Orient Steam Navigation Co. Ltd.
(P&O Bulk Shipping Division, managers), London.
11.3.1980: Commenced oil storage contract at Ardjuna, Indonesia.
1982: Managers became P&O Deep Sea Cargo Division.
1985: Sold through Marubeni (Hong Kong) Ltd. to China National
Metals and Minerals.
27.7.1985: Arrived at Huangpu for demolition.

LAUDERDALE 1978-1982 Ore/oil carrier.
O.N. 358705 143,959g 111,557n 335.67 x 53.68 x 27.51 metres.
Two steam turbines by Mitsubishi Heavy Industries Ltd., Nagasaki,
Japan, double reduction geared to a single screw shaft; 32,000 SHP,
15 knots.
Cargo capacity: 11,260,336 cubic metres liquid.
23.7.1972: Launched by Mitsubishi Heavy Industries Ltd,
Nagasaki, Japan, (Yard No. 1685).
12.2.1972: Delivered to P&O Steam Navigation Company (P&O
Bulk Shipping Division, managers) London as LAUDERDALE.
4.1.1978: Owners became the Orient Steam Navigation Co. Ltd.,
(P&O Bulk Shipping Division, managers), London.

28.5.1982: Sold to Saudi Tankers Ltd., Georgetown, Cayman
Islands (Saudi Maritime Co. Ltd., Jeddah, Saudi Arabia, managers),
renamed ALKISMA ALARABIA and registered in Damman.
1983: Owners became the Arabian International Maritime Co. Ltd.
(AIMCO), Jeddah, Saudi Arabia (Atlas Maritime Company S.A.,
Piraeus, Greece, managers).
1990: Owners became Coldstream Shipping S.A., Monrovia,
Liberia (Arabian International Maritime Co. Ltd., Jeddah, Saudi
Arabia)(Atlas Maritime Company S.A., Piraeus, Greece, managers).
6.5.1994: Arrived at Alang to be broken up by Gem Industries.
28.5.1994: Work began.

NEWFOREST 1983-1985 Bulk carrier

O.N. 705452 83,985g 52,722n 291.7 x 45.17 x 23.02 metres.
Eight-cylinder 2SCSA Burmeister & Wain oil engine by Eriksbergs M/V A/B, Gothenburg, Sweden; 30,400 BHP, 16 knots.
Cargo capacity: 171,192 cubic metres.
16.11.1971: Launched by Eriksbergs M/V A/B (Lindholmen Division), Gothenburg, Sweden. (Yard No. 641)
1972: Completed for Odd Bergs Tankrederi A/S (Odd Berg & Company, managers), Oslo, Norway as the ore/bulk/oil carrier KOLL.
1976: Sold to Utah Transport Inc., Monrovia, Liberia (Utah International Inc., San Francisco, USA) and renamed LAKE TAHOE.

19.10.1983: Acquired by The Orient Steam Navigation Co. Ltd. (P&O Bulk Shipping Ltd., managers), London and renamed NEWFOREST. She served in the fleet only as a bulk carrier.
17.5.1985: Sold to Sweetapple Shipping Ltd., Hong Kong (Astro Marine Inc., New York, USA (Calvin Cheng), managers).
1986: Sold to Joscar Shipping Co. Inc., Manila, Philippines (P&O Bulk Shipping Ltd., London, managers).
1987: Sold to Clutterfield Co. Ltd. (P&O Ship Management (Hong Kong) Ltd., managers), Hong Kong and chartered back to P&O.
1989: Sold to Edi Marine Carriers Ltd., Taipei, Taiwan and renamed OCEAN CAMPAIGNER.
1.12.1993: Arrived Nantong, Jiangsu Province, China to be broken up.

Top opposite: *Irfon* loading ore at Vitoria, Brazil during July 1974.
[National Maritime Museum]

Lower opposite: *Lauderdale.*
[G.R. Scott collection]

Left: *Newforest* as *Koll.*
[World Ship Photo Library]

Below: *Newforest.*
[Fotoflite incorporating Skyfotos]

SHIPS MANAGED FOR THE SHIPPING CONTROLLER
1919-1921

Dates under Orient Line management are shown immediately after name.
All are steel steamers.

RIO NEGRO 1919-1921

O.N. 143078 4,556g 2,879n 361.2 x 46.7 x 26.1 feet

T.3-cyl. by J. C. Tecklenborg A.G., Geestemünde; 334 NHP 1,960 IHP 10.5 knots.

Passengers: 50 first, 230 steerage (*1921:* 80).

20.2.1905: Launched by J. C. Tecklenborg A.G., Geestemünde (Yard No. 201).

19.4.1905: Delivered to Hamburg-Südamerikanische D.G., Hamburg, Germany as RIO NEGRO for Hamburg to Brazil service.

8.1914: Requisitioned by Imperial German Navy as a supply ship.

6.12.1914: Arrived Kiel for conversion into a *Sperrbrecher* (vessel filled with empty drums and sent through mined areas in advance of naval ships).

29.3.1917-27.9.1917: In service as SPERRBRECHER 10.

21.2.1918-9.12.1918: In service as SPERRBRECHER 1.

29.3.1919: Surrendered to the Allied Shipping Controller and allocated to The Shipping Controller, London. Management allocated to Orient Steam Navigation Co. Ltd., London.

29.1.1921: Sold to Ellerman Lines Ltd., Liverpool. Registered at Liverpool and renamed CITY OF PALERMO.

1928: Managers became the Ellerman and Bucknall Steamship Co. Ltd., London.

7.1933: Sold to Italian General Shipping Ltd.

30.8.1933: Arrived at La Spezia for breaking up.

Rio Negro in peacetime colours. *[Peter Newall collection]*

Rio Negro as *Sperrbrecher 10.* *[Prof. Theodor F. Siersdorfer collection]*

Ellerman Lines *City of Palermo,* the last guise of *Rio Negro.* *[Ian Farquhar collection]*

FRIEDRICHSRUH 1919-1921 Twin screw

O.N. 143195 8,332g 5,067n 469.2 x 55.1 x 29.7 feet.

Two Q.4-cyl. by Fairfield Shipbuilding and Engineering Co. Ltd., Glasgow; 783 NHP 14.5 knots.

Passengers: 243 first, 44 second, 1,300 steerage.

22.3.1905: Launched by Fairfield Shipbuilding and Engineering Co. Ltd., Glasgow (Yard No. 438). She had been laid down as WETTIN.

10.6.1905: Delivered to Hamburg-Amerika Paketfahrt A.G., Hamburg, Germany as FUERST BISMARCK for Hamburg to New York service.

31.7.1914: Renamed FRIEDRICHSRUH.

13.9.1917: Requisitioned by the Imperial German Navy.

2.4.1919: Surrendered to the Allied Shipping Controller and allocated to The Shipping Controller (Orient Steam Navigation Co. Ltd., managers), London.

1921: Transferred to French Government.

21.11.1921: Sold to Société des Services Contractuels des Messageries Maritimes, Marseilles, France and renamed AMBOISE.

26.9.1935: Arrived at Genoa for demolition by Alberto Trivero.

Friedrichsruh. [Ian Farquhar collection]

Two views of *Rio Pardo* leaving Cape Town with troops. Whilst the Orient Line flag is flying on her mainmast, on the stern she has the unusual Armistice flag below the British ensign - see also the photo of *Friedrichsruh* on page 23.
[*Ship Society of South Africa/ Martin Leendertz collection*]

RIO PARDO 1919-1921 Twin screw

O.N. 143068 4,588g 2,900n 361.1 x 46.7 x 26.2 feet.
Two T.3-cyl. by J. C. Tecklenborg A.G., Geestemünde; 334 NHP,
1,960 IHP, 10.5 knots.
Passengers: 50 first, 230 steerage (1921: 80).
20.5.1905: Launched by J.C. Tecklenborg A.G., Geestemünde (Yard
No. 204).
25.8.1905: Delivered to Hamburg-Amerika Paketfahrt A.G.,
Hamburg, Germany as DALMATIA.
21.6.1906: Sold to Hamburg-Südamerikanische D.G., Hamburg and
renamed RIO PARDO.
25.3.1917: Requisitioned by the Imperial German Navy and
converted into a *Sperrbrecher.*

25.3.1917-27.9.1917: In service as SPERRBRECHER 4.
21.2.1918-9.12.1918: In service as SPERRBRECHER 1.
14.12.1918: Returned to owners.
25.5.1919: Surrendered to the Allied Shipping Controller and
allocated to The Shipping Controller (Orient Steam Navigation Co.
Ltd., managers), London.
1921: Sold to Ellerman Lines Ltd., Liverpool.   Registered at
Liverpool and renamed CITY OF ALEXANDRIA.
1927: Managers became Ellerman and Bucknall Steamship Co.
Ltd., London.
10.8.1933: Arrived at Queenstown under tow to be demolished at
Haulbowline Dockyard, Ireland by Petersen and Albeck A/S.

Sperrbrecher 4, formerly *Rio Pardo.* [Prof. Theodor F. Siersdorfer collection]

City of Alexandria ex-*Rio Pardo.* [Ships in Focus]

HUNTSGREEN 1919-1921 Twin screw
O.N. 139066 9,144g 5,148n 463.0 x 57.7 x 35.8 feet.
Two Q.4-cyl. by F. Schichau, Danzig; 820 NHP, 6,500 IHP, 14.5 knots.
Passengers: 107 first, 113 second, 132 third.
1907: Laid down as HOHENLOHE.
9.11.1907: Launched by F. Schichau, Danzig (Yard No. 801).
5.1908: Completed for Norddeutscher Lloyd, Bremen, Germany as DERFFLINGER for Bremen to Far East service.
3.8.1914: Disabled by the British in the Suez Canal.
13.10.1914: Expelled from Egyptian waters and captured by HMS FOXHOUND off Port Said. Renamed HUNTSGREEN and managed by F. Green and Co., London as Expeditionary Force Transport No. C8260.

5.1917: Managers became the Union-Castle Mail Steamship Co. Ltd., London.
1919: Managers became the Orient Steam Navigation Co. Ltd., London.
5.1921: Management ceased.
9.1922: Sold to Fisher Alimonda and Co. Ltd., London.
1.1923: Sold to the Crete Shipping Co. Ltd. (Stelp and Leighton Ltd., managers), London.
6.1923: Sold to Norddeutscher Lloyd, Bremen, Germany and name reverted to DERFFLINGER. Rebuilt as two-class ship for Bremen to New York service.
5.1932: Sold to Stern and Co., Essen, Germany.
12.1932: Broken up by the Technical Service Department of Norddeutscher Lloyd at Bremerhaven.

Two views of *Huntsgreen*, the lower at Avonmouth. *[G.R. Scott collection; J. & M. Clarkson]*

Derfflinger. [Prof. Theodor F. Siersdorfer collection]

CORDOBA 1920
O.N. 143095 4,889g 3,173n 376.5 x 46.3 x 27.2 feet
Q.4-cyl. by Reiherstiegwerft Maschinenfabrik, Hamburg; 302 NHP, 10.5 knots
Passengers: 24 first, 400 steerage.
28.10.1895: Launched by Reiherstiegwerft, Hamburg (Yard No. 396).
21.12.1895: Delivered to Hamburg-Südamerikanische D.G., Hamburg, Germany as CORDOBA.

25.2.1918-4.6.1918: In service as SPERRBRECHER 8.
28.3.1919: Surrendered to the Allied Shipping Controller and allocated to The Shipping Controller, London (Easton, Greig and Co., Glasgow, managers).
1920: Managers became the Orient Steam Navigation Co. Ltd., London.
21.5.1920: Caught fire and abandoned off Socotra Island in the Indian Ocean whilst on a voyage from Rangoon to Constantinople with passengers and in ballast.

Sperrbrecher 8, formerly *Cordoba,* the only wartime photograph located of this ship. *[Prof. Theodor F. Siersdorfer collection]*

SHIPS MANAGED DURING
THE SECOND WORLD WAR

Dates under Orient Line management shown immediately after name.
All are steel steamers or motorships.

JOHAN DE WITT 1940-1946 Twin screw
10,355g 6,077n 482.2 x 59.2 x 34.8 feet.
1933: 10,474g 6,105n 506.2 x 59.2 x 34.8 feet.
Two T.3-cyl. by N.V. Werkspoor, Amsterdam; 7,000 IHP, 16.5 knots.
Passengers: 197 first, 120 second, 36 third (1951: 39 first, 748 tourist).
2.5.1919: Launched by N.V. Nederlandsche Scheepsbouw-Maatschappij, Amsterdam (Yard No. 150).
27.7.1920: Completed for N.V. Stoomvaart Maatschappij 'Nederland', Amsterdam, Holland as JOHAN DE WITT.
12.1931-11.1932: Laid up.
4-10.1933: Lengthened by Amsterdamsche Droogdok Maatschappij, Amsterdam.
31.7.1940: Chartered to the Ministry of War Transport (Orient

Steam Navigation Co. Ltd., managers), London as a troop transport retaining a Dutch crew.
12.3.1946: Returned to owners.
15.12.1948: Sold to Compania Maritima del Este S.A., Panama (Goulandris Brothers (Hellas) Ltd., Piraeus) trading as the Greek Line and renamed NEPTUNIA. Mainmast and aft funnel removed.
1954: Owners became Neptunia Shipping Co. Ltd., Panama (Goulandris Brothers (Hellas) Ltd., Piraeus).
2.11.1957: Struck Daunt Rocks and beached in Whitegate Bay whilst entering Cobh during a voyage from Boston to Bremerhaven with passengers and general cargo. Abandoned as a constructive total loss.
14.2.1958: Refloated.
7.3.1958: Arrived under tow in Nieuw Waterweg for demolition by Simons Scheepssloperij, Hendrik-Ido-Ambacht.

Johan de Witt probably photographed at the Tail of the Bank, River Clyde in 1943. *[National Maritime Museum P23045]*

The rebuilt *Neptunia* ex-*Johan de Witt* in Greek Line colours. *[J. and M. Clarkson collection]*

CHRISTIAAN HUYGENS 1940-1945 Twin screw
16,286g 9,755n 551.4 x 68.8 x 36.2 feet.
Two 6-cyl. 2SCSA oil engines by Sulzer Brothers, Winterthur; 11,600 BHP, 16.5 knots.
Passengers: 269 first, 250 second, 62 third, 52 fourth.
28.9.1927: Launched by N.V. Nederlandsche Scheepsbouw-Maatschappij, Amsterdam (Yard No. 186).
25.1.1928: Completed for N.V. Stoomvaart Maatschappij 'Nederland', Amsterdam, Holland as CHRISTIAAN HUYGENS.

21.7.1940: Chartered to the Ministry of War Transport (Orient Steam Navigation Co. Ltd., managers), London as a troop transport retaining a Dutch crew.
1945: Returned to owners.
26.8.1945: Mined near Westkapelle in the River Scheldt and beached on Zuid Steenbank whilst on a voyage from Antwerp to Rotterdam. One person was killed.
5.9.1945: Broke in two.

Christiaan Huygens. The above picture was taken by G. van Mullen on the 26th August 1945 in the River Scheldt near Antwerp only a few hours before the ship struck a mine. The lighthouse-shape structure behind her bridge housed the surface warning radar. By September 1945, when the lower photo was taken, there was obviously no chance of salvaging the *Christiaan Huygens* from the southern Steenbank. Her armament has not been removed and can be clearly seen. *[L. L. von Munching collection]*

129

MARNIX VAN ST ALDEGONDE 1941-1943 Twin screw
19,355g 11,581n 586.2 x 74.8 x 36.1 feet.
Two Sulzer-type 10-cyl. 2SCSA oil engines by Koninklijke
Maatschappij 'De Schelde', Vlissingen; 14,000 BHP, 16.75 knots.
Passengers: 336 first, 281 second, 64 third.
21.12.1929: Launched by N.V. Nederlandsche Scheepsbouw-
Maatschappij, Amsterdam (Yard No. 195).
10.9.1930: Completed for N.V. Stoomvaart Maatschappij
'Nederland', Amsterdam, Holland as MARNIX VAN ST
ALDEGONDE.

7.5.1941: Chartered to the Ministry of War Transport (Orient Steam
Navigation Co. Ltd., managers), London as troop transport retaining
a Dutch crew.
6.11.1943: Torpedoed by German aircraft six miles off Cape
Bougaroni, Algeria whilst on a voyage in convoy KMF 25A from
Liverpool to North Africa with 3,235 troops for Operation Torch,
the landings in North Africa.
7.11.1943: Sank under tow in position 37.07 north by 6.37 east. No
lives were lost.

Above: *Marnix van St Aldegonde* in peacetime colours.
Below: Troops being ferried ashore in November 1943 during Operation Torch, shortly before *Marnix van St Aldegonde* was torpedoed.
[Upper: Peter Newall collection; lower: Imperial War Museum A12705A]

JOHAN VAN OLDENBARNEVELDT 1940-1945 Twin screw
19,428g 11,605n 586.2 x 74.8 x 36.1 feet.
Two 10-cyl. 2SCSA oil engines by Sulzer Brothers, Winterthur;
14,000 BHP, 16.75 knots.
Passengers: 245-300 first, 246-367 second, 64 third, 60 fourth
(*1951:* 1,144 single class).
3.8.1929: Launched by N.V. Nederlandsche Scheepsbouw-
Maatschappij, Amsterdam (Yard No. 194).
13.3.1930: Completed for N.V. Stoomvaart Maatschappij
'Nederland', Amsterdam, Holland as JOHAN VAN
OLDENBARNEVELDT.
31.7.1940: Chartered to the Ministry of War Transport (Orient
Steam Navigation Co. Ltd., managers), London as a troop transport
retaining a Dutch crew.

12.3.1946: Returned to owners.
6.1951-1.1952: Refitted as single-class ship by N.V. Nederlandsche
Scheepsbouw-Maatschappij and Amsterdamsche Droogdok
Maatschappij, Amsterdam.
1-3.1959: Refitted by Amsterdamsche Droogdok Maatschappij,
Amsterdam. Funnels raised in height and mainmast removed.
8.3.1962: Handed over at Genoa to Shipping Investment
Corporation, Panama trading as the Greek Line, and renamed
LAKONIA under the Greek flag.
22.12.1963: Caught fire 150 miles north east of Madeira in position
35.00 north by 15.15 west whilst on a Christmas cruise from
Southampton to Madeira. 128 lives were lost.
29.12.1963: Capsized and sank whilst under tow about 250 miles
west of Gibraltar in position 35.56 north by 10.00 west.

Johan van Oldenbarneveldt at Singapore prior to her charter by the Ministry of War Transport. Photographed on 29th April 1940
by Dr P. Ransome-Wallis. *[National Maritime Museum N35056]*

Johan van Oldenbarneveldt during the period 1943 to 1945, probably in Liverpool. *[National Maritime Museum G3914]*

SAMKANSA 1943-1947

O.N. 169656 7,265g 4,454n 423.9 x 57.0 x 34.8 feet.
T.3-cyl. by Harrisburg Machinery Corporation, Harrisburg; 2,500 IHP, 11 knots.
25.9.1943: Launched by Bethlehem-Fairfield Shipyard Inc., Baltimore (Yard No. 2240) as NIKOLA TESLA.
4.10.1943: Delivered to United States War Shipping Administration, Washington as SAMKANSA and bareboat chartered to the Ministry of War Transport (Orient Steam Navigation Co. Ltd., managers), London.
1947: Managers became the General Steam Navigation Co. Ltd., London.
17.4.1947: Sold to Hadley Shipping Co. Ltd., London and renamed

CERINTHUS. Chartered to Houlder Brothers.
11.1951: Sold to Rio Amado Compania Naviera S.A., Panama (Capeside Steamship Co. Ltd., London, managers) and renamed PHASSA.
1953: Sold to Compania de Navegacion Cerro La Plata, Panama (Coulothros Ltd., London, managers) and renamed URANIA.
1960: Syros Shipping Co. Ltd. (L. M. Valmas and Son), London became managers.
1964: Sold to Evergreen Navigation Corporation, Monrovia (Wah Kwong and Co., Hong Kong, managers) and renamed CONCORD VENTURE under the Panama flag.
10.1.1970: Arrived at Tadotsu to be broken up by Miyachi Salvage Co. Ltd.

One of two Liberty ships managed by Orient Line, *Samkansa* arriving at Cardiff, possibly in 1947, and still with her wartime life rafts.
[Welsh Industrial and Maritime Museum 1033/1134]

Samkansa as *Cerinthus. [J. and M. Clarkson collection]*

132

SAMEVERON 1944-1947

O.N. 169782 7,274g 4,444n 423.9 x 57.0 x 34.8 feet
T.3-cyl. by General Machinery Corporation, Hamilton, Ohio; 2,500 IHP, 11 knots.
7.1.1944: Launched by Bethlehem-Fairfield Shipyard Inc., Baltimore (Yard No. 2307).
17.1.1944: Delivered to United States War Shipping Administration, Washington as SAMEVERON and bareboat chartered to the Ministry of War Transport (Orient Steam Navigation Co. Ltd., managers), London.
1947: Managers became Trinder, Anderson and Co., London.

18.4.1947: Sold to Bank Line Ltd., London and renamed ERICBANK.
1959: Sold to The People's Republic of China and renamed NAN HAI 146.
1967: Probably renamed HONG QI 146 during the Cultural Revolution.
1974: Ownership transferred to China Ocean Shipping Co., China although the owner was more likely to have been the Bureau of Maritime Transport Administration, Guangzhou Branch.
1992: Deleted from 'Lloyd's Register'.

Above: *Sameveron* at Cape Town. *[World Ship Society Photo Library]*

Below: *Sameveron* as *Ericbank* leaving Dunedin. *[Ian Farquhar]*

EMPIRE DOON/EMPIRE ORWELL 1945-1958 Twin screw
O.N. 180806 16,662g 9,572n (1949: 18,036g 9,946n) 547.8 x 72.5
x 31.5 feet.
Six geared steam turbines by Blohm und Voss, Hamburg; 14,200
SHP, 4,050 NHP, 18 knots.
1973: Two 6-cyl. 4SCSA oil engines by M.A.N., Augsburg; 12,000
BHP, 17 knots.
Passengers: 152 first, 338 tourist (*1949:* 1,491 troops *1959:* 106
first, 2,000 third).
16.7.1936: Launched by Blohm und Voss, Hamburg (Yard No. 506).
4.12.1936: Completed for Deutsche Ost-Afrika-Linie, Hamburg,
Germany as PRETORIA.
29.11.1939: Requisitioned by German Navy as submarine tender.
1.1940: Tender for Second U-Flotille.
12.1940: Accommodation ship for First Submarine Training
Division, Pillau.
22. 2.1945: Hospital ship in Baltic. Used in the evacuation of East
Prussia.
5.1945: Taken over by British Government at Hamburg.

12.11.1945: Handed over to the Ministry of Transport (Orient Steam
Navigation Co. Ltd., managers), London. Refitted at Newcastle-
upon-Tyne and renamed EMPIRE DOON.
5.1947-11.1949: Converted into a troopship by John I. Thornycroft
and Co. Ltd., Southampton.
10.1948: Renamed EMPIRE ORWELL.
11.1959: Sold to the Ocean Steam Ship Co. Ltd. (Alfred Holt and
Co., managers), Liverpool, converted into a pilgrim ship by Barclay,
Curle and Co. Ltd., Glasgow and renamed GUNUNG DJATI.
3.1962: Sold to Indonesian Government and registered under the
ownership of P.T.Pelajaran Nasional Indonesia.
1964: Sold to P.T. Maskapi Pelajaran Sang Saka.
7.1965: Sold to P.T.Perusahaan Pelajaran 'Arafat', Djakarta,
Indonesia
4-10.1973: Refitted by Hongkong United Dockyards, Hong Kong
and converted to a motorship.
1979: Following liquidation of owners, sold to Indonesian Navy and
renamed TANJUNG PANDAN (Pennant No. 971).
1987: Reported sold for scrap in Taiwan.

Pretoria in her distinctive DOAL guise (above) and as the troopship *Empire Doon* (below).
[Above: G.R. Scott collection; below: National Maritime Museum G6590]

Left *Empire Orwell,* minus funnel and lifeboats, whilst being refitted by Thornycroft at Southampton. Her boilers were replaced and engines modified.
[World Ship Photo Library] Interior views of the ship appear on pages 166-167.

Below: *Empire Orwell* berthed at Southampton on 19th August 1951 in almost pristine condition prior to a three and half month tour of duty to the Far East.
[World Ship Society Photo Library]

Right: *Gunung Djati* sails from the Clyde in Blue Funnel colours after her conversion to a pilgrim ship.
[Glasgow City Libraries and Archives T-RK 59/119/7]

This aerial view of the Tilbury landing stage was taken on 28th May 1930, twelve days after it was officially opened. Now a listed building, much of the main baggage hall and the landing platform survives although there is no longer a rail link to the terminal. Note the 17th century Tilbury Fort in the background. A cross-section of the landing stage is shown top right. *[Simmons Aerofilms Ltd. 32061]*

Taken on 19th June 1930, this photo of the Centre Branch Dock shows four of the post-war 20,000-tonners laid up during the European summer when it was too hot to transit the Suez Canal. These ships were usually employed during this period on Northern Europe or Mediterranean cruises. In the distance is Gravesend Reach, the original dock entrance and tidal basin, a P&O liner in the large dry dock, the landing stage and the Tilbury Hotel. *[Simmons Aerofilms Ltd. 32802]*

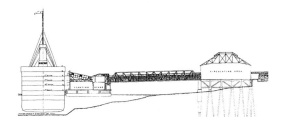

THE ORIENT LINE AND TILBURY

Since its formation, Orient Line was always a London company. The West Indies traders operated in and out of the West India Docks whilst the Australian ships including the 1879-built *Orient*, the largest ship in the world after the *Great Eastern*, sailed from the South West India Docks. At that time the various docks in London were privately owned and competition for trade was fierce. The three West India Docks and the nearby East India Docks were controlled by the East and West India Dock Company. Their greatest rival was the London and St. Katherine Docks Company which opened its large Royal Albert Dock for business in 1880. This move prompted the East and West India Dock Company to set in motion a bold plan for new docks to be built on marshland at Tilbury, some twenty-six miles down river from London Bridge.

The new port would be opposite Gravesend, the traditional quarantine station, landing and embarkation point for passengers travelling to and from London. Ships were able to navigate to Gravesend Reach on the River Thames at all states of the tide and anchor mid stream where the Gravesend to Tilbury ferries, operated by the London Tilbury and Southend Railway Company, were used as passenger tenders. The ability of ships to come so far up river in most conditions was also one of the great advantages of Tilbury. Unlike the docks up river, with their huge warehouses, Tilbury was the first truly modern London dock facility designed for rapid transportation of goods. With electrically lit quays, sheds for short-term storage, sixty-one travelling cranes and an extensive railway network connected to the London Tilbury and Southend line, this far-sighted scheme also included land set aside to the west for future dock extensions.

The 700-feet entrance lock could easily accommodate the largest ship in the world at that time whilst the large tidal basin had two berths, 28 and 29, for passenger arrivals and departures, each with baggage sheds, waiting areas and railway platforms serving Fenchurch Street and Liverpool Street Stations. Opposite these berths stood the large five-storey Tilbury Hotel with its distinctive half-timbered front overlooking the Thames (see the photograph

of *Orontes* (1) on page 77). With accommodation for 110 guests the hotel was fitted out by Maple and Company and was designed for the numerous passengers using the new docks. Along with Tilbury Fort, the Tilbury Hotel remained a feature of the Tilbury skyline until it was destroyed by a German incendiary bomb on the 4th February 1944.

Soon after work commenced in July 1882, problems were encountered excavating the large area of waterlogged land. Costs soared from the original estimate of £1.1 million to £2.75 million on completion of the docks in 1886. The opening ceremony took place on 17th April 1886 when the London, Tilbury and Southend Railway Company ferry *Tilbury* (269/1883) with dignitaries aboard cut through the ribbon at the main entrance. Glen Line's *Glenfruin* (2,985/1880) soon followed as the first ocean-going ship to enter the new docks. The euphoria of the grand opening was short-lived, however, as the projected new trade did not materialise. This was partly due to traditional working practices in the old docks conflicting with new ways at Tilbury. Shipping companies were also unwilling to make the move without financial inducements. The over-stretched East and West India Dock Company was forced therefore to offer companies large rate reductions and although finances improved gradually, in 1888 the dock company was placed in the hands of receivers who oversaw the operation until 1893.

Clan Line moved to Tilbury in August 1886 and in January 1887 Orient Line arrived with the brand-new *Ormuz* (1) taking the first sailing on 3rd February 1887. Despite the dock improvements, passengers continued to be embarked, depending on the tide, by tender right up to the early 1900s. A special Orient Line boat train also ran from Fenchurch Street Station (not far from the Orient Line offices at 5 Fenchurch Avenue) although this was later switched to St. Pancras Station.

By the end of the century the docks had turned the corner with total tonnage exceeding one million for the first time and in 1901 the East and West India Dock Company and the London and St. Katherine Docks Company merged to form the London and India Docks Company. On 31st March 1909 all the privately owned London docks were nationalised and brought under the control of the newly formed Port of London Authority (P.L.A.). At the time London docks were the largest in the world with an annual tonnage of vessels approaching 39 million.

The formation of the P.L.A. coincided with Orient Line's 1909 expansion programme and with the increased size of ships using Tilbury, the port authority began an extensive series of dock improvements. Work started in 1912 on an extension of the Main Dock which was only completed in 1917 because of the outbreak of war. Three new berths were completed on the south side, 31 to 33, and these were used mainly by Orient Line and P&O. In 1926 construction commenced on a new 750-feet dry dock to the east of the original dry docks (see *Orion* page 101) and a new 1,000-feet entrance lock to the west of the main docks. The latter was designed to more than adequately receive the largest ships afloat at that time. On 17th September 1929 the new

The Tilbury to Gravesend paddle ferry *Thames* (125/1868) alongside *Ormuz* (1) in the 1890s. The local ferries were often used as tenders for ships anchored midstream in the Thames. *Thames* was built in Liverpool and was bought by the London Tilbury and Southend Railway Company in 1882 and scrapped in 1913.

[Peter Newall collection]

dry dock was opened and nine days later, on 26th September, *Oronsay* (1) marked the official opening of the new lock when Lady Ritchie, wife of the PLA chairman, pressed a lever aboard the ship which opened the road and rail bascule bridge at the entrance to the lock. The ship then entered the lock and cut the ribbon across the gates leading into the Main Dock.

1926 also saw work start on a new passenger landing stage at Tilbury. This extraordinary structure, which is still in use today, consists of a 1,142-foot floating platform attached to the shore by four massive hinged booms and heavy mooring cable which allow for fluctuations of up to 20 feet in the tides. The depth of water also enables vessels to come alongside at any state of the tide. At the eastern end of the landing stage 300 feet was reserved for the London Midland and Scottish Railway Company's ferry service between Tilbury and Gravesend. A large customs and baggage hall was also built plus an enlarged railway station, which offered frequent train services into London. The Prime Minister Sir Ramsay MacDonald opened the landing stage on 16th May 1930 with P&O's *Mongolia* (16,504/1923), the first ship to embark passengers.

Apart from the loss of the Tilbury Hotel, Tilbury Docks suffered relatively little damage during the Second World War. In the early 1950s the Main Dock was widened to 900 feet to allow more manoeuvring space for the new post-war Orient and P&O liners. A new 842-foot quay (Number One Berth) and passenger terminal were also constructed from 1954 to 1957 at the south end of the West Branch Dock to accommodate these larger ships. The new terminal cost £1.6 million and contained spacious waiting areas, its own railway platform, a viewing gallery for friends and relatives and a large covered car park. Alas, it was all too late and in 1960 Orient Line's largest and latest ship *Oriana*, although registered at London, became the first Orient liner to make Southampton her homeport. In October 1969, three years after Orient was absorbed, P&O moved its liners from Tilbury to Southampton thus bringing to an end 82 years of its passenger operations at the port.

Top: Dressed overall, *Oronsay* (1) opened the new Tilbury entrance dock on 26th September 1929. The bascule bridge is raised and she is about to enter the 1,000-foot lock.
[Ian Farquhar collection]

Right: *Oronsay* (2) alongside Number One Berth in the 1960s.

Below: *Orion* at the Tilbury landing stage during the 1950s. The ferry is *Catherine* (259/1903), one of four vessels built early in the twentieth century for the Tilbury to Gravesend service. She and two of her running mates remained on the service until they were sold for demolition in 1961.   *[Peter Newall collection]*

AUSTRALIAN CONNECTIONS

As the principal shipping line between Britain and Australia, Orient Line developed many business interests in Australia including a share in Australian National Airways, a stevedoring company and the agencies for numerous firms. The company, with its significant amount of reefer space, was also heavily involved in assisting the development of Australian chilled meat, butter and fruit exports.

'Australian Annals' was compiled in 1946 by Orient Line staff in Australia as "a collection of what, to some of us here, seem to be items of interest connected principally with the Australian end of the Orient Line business." This unpublished document contains a wealth of interesting information about the company and below are some of the key facts concerning the operation at the various ports.

ADELAIDE
Largs Bay 1877-1908
Until the opening of the Outer Harbour at Adelaide in 1908, Orient Line ships made nearby Largs Bay their Australian port of call. The anchorage was about two miles out from the Government Jetty at Semaphore, which was the drop-off point for the mails. Semaphore Jetty was about two miles from Port Adelaide and until January 1878 there was no railway link between the two places and the journey had to be undertaken by horse-drawn omnibus. In December 1882 the privately owned jetty at Largs Bay was completed, about a mile north of the one at Semaphore, and connected with the railway, which now ran between Semaphore and Port Adelaide. Passengers were landed at the new jetty from February 1883 whilst mails continued to use Semaphore Jetty until 1887 when Largs Bay Jetty became the landing place for both mail and passengers.

Lusitania made the first Orient Line call at Largs Bay, homeward bound, on 17th September 1877. After a stay of three days loading wool and other merchandise as well as coal for her bunkers, she sailed for England. A few days later on 25th September *Chimborazo* arrived from the UK and made the first outward bound call at Adelaide.

Outer Harbour
The Outer Harbour was opened on 16th January 1908 and the first Orient liners to berth in the new harbour were the homeward *Oruba* on the opening day and *Orotava* outward, on 20th January. The last ship to use Largs Bay was *Ormuz* (1) on 6th January. Sydney and Melbourne Mails were also landed and embarked here.

Adelaide offices
Between 1877 and 1887 an agency, J.Stilling and Co., represented the company in Adelaide. The first Orient Line office opened in 1887 at 28 Grenfell Street with M.G. Anderson, the acting branch manager. In 1901 the branch office closed and M.G. Anderson became the company agent with his firm M.G. Anderson and Co. In 1946 when 'Australian Annals' was written, he still operated in that capacity.

(877) ALONGSIDE THE WHARF AT THE OUTER HARBOUR—ADELAIDE.

AN ORIENT LINER AT THE OUTER HARBOUR—ADELAIDE. (2411)

(2523) EMBARKING MAILBAGS FROM THE SYDNEY AND MELBOURNE MAIL TRAIN AT THE OUTER HARBOUR—ADELAIDE.

GETTING MAILS ON DECK READY TO LAND AT ADELAIDE. (1570)

Otranto (1) at Adelaide circa 1910-1914 from 'A voyage with the mails'.

BRISBANE

Extension to Brisbane

Although Orient had a contract with the Queensland Government to carry migrants from London via Sydney, the service was only extended to Brisbane in 1905. *Orotava* was the first ship to visit the port on 2nd September 1905.

Berthing arrangements

Orient ships initially berthed at Pinkenba Wharf at the mouth of the Brisbane River, about twelve miles from the city. On 15th September 1913, starting with *Orvieto*, the berth was moved ten miles up river to New Farm Wharf. This arrangement changed permanently on 29th October 1935 when *Orsova* (1) moved to the berth at Hamilton.

Brisbane offices

Between 1877 and 1926, the local agent for Orient Line was B.D. Morehead and Co. (Moreheads Ltd. in 1899). In 1926 a branch office was established at the corner of Queen and Eagle Streets and in 1930 the company had its own building, which was constructed in 1929-1930, at 113-119 Eagle Street.

Orontes (1) at Pinkenba Wharf, Brisbane. *[Peter Newall collection]*

Orsova (1) leaving New Farm Wharf, Brisbane. *[Peter Newall collection]*

MELBOURNE

Hobson's Bay anchorage 1878-1882

Starting with *Aconcagua* on 5th July 1878, ships initially anchored in Hobson's Bay and cargo was worked with lighters.

Williamstown Railway Pier 1882-1891

On 12th October 1882 *Liguria* was the first to berth at the Williamstown Railway Pier which was also the berth for P&O. Williamstown is a suburb south west of Melbourne. During this period urgent despatch ships continued to use the Hobson's Bay anchorage.

Port of Melbourne

Because the Williamstown Railway Pier was occupied, *Oroya* berthed at the Port of Melbourne Railway Pier on 4th June 1891. There also had been problems with the depth of water at Williamstown. In April 1916 the Melbourne base became the new Prince's Pier in the Port of Melbourne. This arrangement changed when the nearby Station Pier was open for traffic with *Otranto* (2) on 15th September 1930. *Oronsay* (1) almost opened Station Pier unofficially on 10th December 1929 when she broke loose from her mooring at Prince's Pier during a strong wind and was only saved through the prompt reaction of her captain.

Sailing day at Melbourne for *Otranto* (1).

Melbourne offices

Bright Bros. and Co. was the Melbourne agent between 1877 and 1888. The company's first office was in the Robert's Building, 137 Collins Street in 1888. In 1898 it moved to The Equitable Life Building, Collins Street and in 1924 the company purchased its own building at 356 Collins Street.

A busy scene at the Railway Pier, Melbourne with *Otranto* (1) alongside.

SYDNEY
Berthing arrangements
Orient ships were first berthed on the west side of Circular Quay but in 1883 this was changed to the east side. In June 1924 No.7 Wharf, Woolloomooloo Bay became the company's permanent berth with *Osterley*, the first user. No.8 Wharf, Woolloomooloo Bay was used when two ships were in port. Between 1886 and 1912 the company owned a small launch/tug *Estrella* which was used as a passenger ferry and to tow company lighters. Occasionally she also became a pleasure launch for Orient Line staff and friends with trips round the harbour and picnics served aboard.

Sydney offices
Between 1877 and 1881 the company was represented by Gilchrist Watt and Co. The first office from 1881 to 1885 was at 267 George Street. A move took place in 1885 to 39

Orient Line offices, Sydney. The building on the left was demolished in 1939 and replaced by the one on the right. *[P&O Archives]*

Pitt Street followed by 12 Martin Place in 1902. In 1917 Orient purchased its own building at 2-4-6 Spring Street. In 1939 this classical-style building with its arched windows and triangular pediments was pulled down and replaced with a magnificent modern building designed by local architects in association with Brian O' Rorke. Completed in 1940 the new Orient Line Building attracted much favourable comment and won two prestigious architectural prizes. The style also reflected the new clean modern look of *Orion* and *Orcades* (2). The exterior was unpretentious with the ground floor and mezzanine faced with travertine and granite whilst the floors above were

Orford passing under the partly-completed Sydney Harbour Bridge on 18th December 1930. She also took part in the opening of the bridge on 19th March 1932.
[J. and M. Clarkson collection]

sandstone with architraves of Portland stone specially brought over from England. The interior colour scheme was blue and coral and the main booking hall featured glass panels designed by Lynton Lamb who also created the fine glasswork on *Orion* and *Orcades* (2) - these are currently on display in the entrance to the Passengers Gallery in the Australian Maritime Museum, Sydney. A large model of *Orontes* (2) was also featured in the show window at the entrance to the building, which was unfortunately demolished in 1988.

TASMANIA
Hobart
Orient Line ships called regularly in Tasmania during the apple season. The first vessel was *Iberia* on 25th March 1889 when she loaded 7,029 cases of apples for London at the old Dunn Street Pier. On 4th March 1910 King's Pier was opened with *Orontes* (2) alongside and this berth was used until 1914 when the Ocean Pier became the regular Orient berth with the arrival of *Osterley* on 13th March.
Burnie
Frequent stops at Burnie were made during the summer months commencing with *Orford* on 3rd December 1935.
Agencies
In Hobart, Macfarlane Bros. and Co. were appointed as the company agent in 1877 whilst at Burnie the agent appointed in 1935 was the Van Diemen's Land Co.

WESTERN AUSTRALIA
Albany
Before the discovery of gold in 1891, the population of

Western Australia was relatively small but by the end of the decade, it had more than trebled to almost 180,000. Regular calls were made at Albany and from the early 1890s the company did its own lightering with the tug *Escort* towing the lighter *Camilla*.
Fremantle
Fremantle Harbour was completed in August 1900 and Albany ceased to be the port of call for Western Australia. *Ormuz* (1) was the first Orient liner to arrive at Victoria Wharf, Fremantle that August.
Western Australia offices
Between 1887 and 1892 the Orient agency in Albany was J. McKail and Co. and this was changed to W.G. Knight and Son from 1892 to 1896 when the company established its own office. After the move to Fremantle in 1900, it reverted to an agency.

The agents at Fremantle and Perth between 1887 and 1900 were J. Lilley and Co. (Perth: 1896-1900 Forrest, Emanuel and Co.). In 1900 separate offices were established at Phillimore Street, Fremantle and Barrack Street, Perth. In 1903 the Perth office moved to 105 St. George's Terrace and in 1930 Orient Line moved to its own building which had been erected at 56-60 William Street. The company was also the focal point for Western Australia air passenger and freight bookings from 1936 as it was the principal agent for Adelaide Airways and its successor Australian National Airways (taken over by Ansett Airways in 1957) in which Orient Line had a major shareholding.

Hobart circa 1910. *[Peter Newall collection]*

THE ORIENT LINE AND BARROW-IN-FURNESS

The close relationship between Vickers-Armstrongs Ltd., Barrow-in-Furness and Orient Line lasted almost 40 years and resulted in some of the finest liners ever built in Britain.

Orama (2), the first of the new post-war series, was launched on 20th May 1924 by Miss Winifred Cook, daughter of the Australian High Commissioner, Sir Joseph Cook. Although she was intended to be named *Oriana*, she was instead named after the ship which had been torpedoed and sunk in 1917. *Orama* (2) is distinguished from her near sisters by the plated-in upper forward superstructure. *[Sankeys Ltd.]*

At the final stages of completion in the Buccleuch Dock, *Orama* (2) was one of the first liners to be fitted with the new Maclachlan gravity davit instead of the traditional turn out Welin-type davit. Note also the docking bridge on her stern and the overhang of B deck. *[Sankeys Ltd.]*

143

Above: The 1925 *Oronsay* (1) was the only post-war Orient passenger ship not built by Vickers. The first in the fleet over 20,000gt, she was constructed by John Brown on the Clyde. Here she is seen at Barrow probably in the mid 1930s having her capacity reduced from 1,780 to 983 passengers. *[Sankeys Ltd.]*

Left: *Otranto* (2) prior to her launch in June 1925. Like all the 1920s Barrow-built ships she was registered at Barrow. Her twin screws were driven by two sets of Parsons-type geared turbines. Below is one of the sets consisting of a low-pressure ahead and astern turbine; low-pressure ahead and high-pressure astern turbine and high-presure ahead turbine. *[Sankeys Ltd.]*

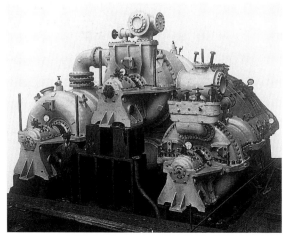

Orford, the fourth of the 20,000-tonners, was launched on 27th September 1927 by Lady Ryde, wife of the Australian High Commissioner. Note the difference between her forward superstructure and that of *Orama* (2) shown on page 143. *[Sankeys Ltd.]*

Above: The final ship in the series, *Orontes* (2) was completed in September 1929. Instead of a straight stem, she was given a soft-nose raked bow. *[Sankeys Ltd.]*

Below: When *Orion* was launched on 1st December 1934 she had a traditional Orient Line black hull. As *Orama* (2) had not returned from Australia on her experimental voyage with a corn-coloured hull, the company was still undecided about *Orion's* paint scheme. *[Sankeys Ltd.]*

Above: *Orion* received her new colours during fitting-out. Here the newly-completed ship is passing the Buccleuch Dock bridge.
[*Sankeys Ltd.*]

Left: In 1935 *Orford* returned to Barrow for changes to her accommodation layout.
[*Sankeys Ltd.*]

Below: Launched on 7th December 1936 by Mrs Irvine Geddes, wife of the chairman of Orient Line, *Orcades* (2) with her taller funnel was a tidied-up version of *Orion*. Her thicker and more widely spaced stanchions gave the ship cleaner lines and became a feature of all P&O and Orient liners up to *Oriana* and *Canberra*. [*Sankeys Ltd.*]

Above: *Orcades* (2) after completion in 1937.   [*Sankeys Ltd.*]

Left: *Orcades* (2) developed engine trouble during a Mediterranean cruise and returned to Barrow for a three-month refit on 18th May 1939. Here she is in July with her funnel covered.   In August she was requisitioned as a troop transport.
[*National Maritime Museum N36212*]

Below: Lost during the war, *Orcades* (2) was replaced by a new *Orcades* (3).   Here she is during the final stages of construction in 1947.
[*Peter Newall collection*]

Orcades (3) was launched on 14th October 1947 by Lady Morshead, wife of Sir Leslie, Orient Line's General Manager in Australia. Note the recess for her anchor. Prior to the launch Lady Morshead was shown the launching mechanism by the foreman shipwright. *Orcades'* funnel was placed in position during fitting out. *[Top and middle: Peter Newall collection; bottom: Sankeys Ltd.]*

On 28th October 1950 the 27,632gt *Oronsay* (2) caught fire whilst fitting-out in the Buccleuch Dock. The blaze lasted 32 hours before it was brought under control. Despite a heavy list to port, the ship was saved from capsizing by lowering the water level in the dock and flooding the starboard tanks. Remarkably, her completion was only delayed by two months and she was delivered in May 1951. *[Sankeys Ltd.]*

Top: *Orsova* (2) was the last of the trio of post-war ships and arguably the most attractive of all the Orient liners. She was the culmination of a design started with *Orion* twenty years earlier.

Right: *Oriana,* on the other hand, was another design break with the past which produced a unique ship. Her keel was laid on 18th September 1957 and building took over three years.

Below: When completed in 1960, *Oriana* was not only the largest liner built in England to that date but also, like many of her Orient Line predecessors, the largest ship to operate between Britain and Australia.

[All: Sankeys Ltd.]

Above: The 'Orient Guide' was published regularly in the late nineteenth century and described the journey to and from Australia as well as scenes aboard plus deck plans of the various ships. From the 1888 edition is this artist's impression of the promenade deck on *Orizaba* and *Oroya*. Note the small cannon below the bridge. This was required by the 1873 Merchant Shipping Act and was only used as a distress signal.

Below: The 1888 'Orient Guide' also shows the magnificent first-class dining saloon on *Ormuz* (1) with the carved coat of arms in the background.

LIFE ABOARD

For over a 100 years Orient Line carried thousands of passengers between Britain and Australia and was often seen as the premier carrier between the motherland and the new territories in the southern hemisphere. From gold prospectors in the 1850s to the 'ten pound poms' of the post-Second World War era, many of the passengers travelled in relatively simple accommodation whereas first class tended to be the domain of the entrepreneurs, civil servants and colonial administrators.

Because of the long distances involved, travel by sailing ship to Australia continued into the latter part of the nineteenth century and well after steam had taken over the trade on other migrant routes. Whilst a small number travelled in saloon class in the poop, the majority had to make do with temporary accommodation in the 'tween decks which was then removed for the journey home and the space used for cargoes such as wool. The iron clipper *Harbinger* of 1876 was one of a series of fine sailing ships owned by Orient and the last to be specially built for the Australian passenger trade.

On the first 1870s-built Pacific Steam Navigation Company (P.S.N.C.) steamships operated by Orient Line, first class was situated aft, like the sailing ships, in what was known as first saloon whilst second saloon was amidships. This arrangement changed in 1879 with the arrival of the company's first purpose-built steamship, *Orient* (2), which at the time was one of the largest ships in the world. On this vessel the first class dining room was forward on the main deck between the main and foremast and occupied the entire width of the ship with a skylight in front of the bridge.

Although first class on *Orient* (2) had the use of an 160-feet long promenade deck, the deck space was very cluttered with machinery and rigging for the auxiliary sails. The ship was also narrow with a beam of only 35 feet and during hot weather every effort was made to alleviate the humidity below decks. This view was taken in 1885 during the Suez Canal transit on *Orient* (2) before she was fitted with a raised forecastle. Note the ship's bell, and ladies in their bonnets and crinoline outfits. The other photograph (top right) is the view looking aft towards the first class promenade and mainmast with topsails set. *[National Maritime Museum: bottom C4880 (11); top C4880 (9)]*

Austral

In 1881 P&O's response to *Orient* (2) was a pair of liners just over 5,000gt, *Rome* and *Carthage,* the largest ships to that date owned by P&O. Orient Line meanwhile had ordered an enlarged version of *Orient* (2), the 5,589gt *Austral,* its first steel-hulled ship, which entered service in 1882. The new ship featured a number of innovations such as baths, electric light throughout the ship and a four-foot wide corridor on the main deck running between the passenger accommodation and the side of the ship (right). This allowed easy access through the ship without passing through the dining saloons and also enabled staterooms to have windows instead of portholes which could be opened even during rough weather. Air circulation was improved with the opening of portholes on the seaward side of the corridor whilst the painted glass windows of the first-class dining saloon could be lowered at will. The seating arrangements in this walnut-panelled room consisted of two long tables in the centre with smaller tables port and starboard and long banquette seats running fore and aft (top and below). During the 1883/4 rebuilding of the ship after its sinking at Sydney in 1882, the main deck corridor was removed and the space used to increase the number of staterooms, with the 120-capacity first-class saloon extended to the full width of the ship.

[All: Peter Newall collection]

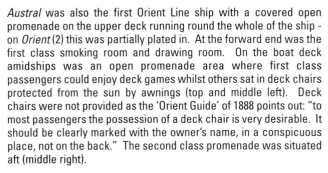

Austral was also the first Orient Line ship with a covered open promenade on the upper deck running round the whole of the ship - on *Orient* (2) this was partially plated in. At the forward end was the first class smoking room and drawing room. On the boat deck amidships was an open promenade area where first class passengers could enjoy deck games whilst others sat in deck chairs protected from the sun by awnings (top and middle left). Deck chairs were not provided as the 'Orient Guide' of 1888 points out: "to most passengers the possession of a deck chair is very desirable. It should be clearly marked with the owner's name, in a conspicuous place, not on the back." The second class promenade was situated aft (middle right).

Passenger baggage allowances were very generous and were measured in cubic feet: 40 per first class passenger; 20 second class and 15 third. Items "not wanted on board" were stowed in the baggage room via one of the small holds (right).

[Top: Peter Newall collection; National Maritime Museum: middle left C4880 (5); middle right C4880 (3); bottom right C4880 (4)]

H. M. S. OPHIR

Ophir

In 1901 *Ophir* was chartered as a royal yacht for a seven-month tour of the colonies by the Duke and Duchess of Cornwall and York (later King George V and Queen Mary). After a two-month refit at Tilbury, she emerged as *HMS Ophir* in February. These images show her as a royal yacht.

Right: Promenade deck.

Below: Situated between the funnel casings was the impressive Royal Dining Room with its barrel-vaulted, stained glass roof. This view facing aft shows the Turkish carpets, Chippendale-style chairs and in the arched space of the dome, the shields of the leading Australian colonies with figures representing their industries. Note the kangaroos in the left-hand corner of the arch.

Top: On the promenade deck forward was the delightful Royal Drawing Room, which was panelled in rosewood and satinwood with Sheraton-style satinwood furniture upholstered in blue and white silk damask. The deep pile carpet was fawn coloured.

Bottom left: Entrance to the Royal Drawing Room.

Bottom right: At the forward end of the upper deck were the Royal Apartments. The Duke and Duchess had separate suites, each with its own bathroom, bedroom and sitting room. This is Duchess's sitting room which, like all the Royal Apartments, was painted white.

[Badge: Paul Louden-Brown collection;
all photographs: Peter Newall collection]

NEW TWIN-SCREW STEAMSHIP, "Omrah,"

Omrah

Omrah of 1899 was the final and largest Orient passenger ship completed in the nineteenth century and the first to be purpose-built with a single funnel. She also epitomised the late Victorian British liner with an ornate first class dining saloon rising three decks and lit from above by a large dome skylight (below). Classical columns punctuated the overall design whilst the sides of the saloon were panelled in inlaid rosewood and mahogany. The swivel chairs allowed easy access at the long dining tables whilst music was provided by an organ at the forward end. Passenger cabins, on the other hand, were relatively cramped, even in first class (right). The Pullman-style bunks had curtains and metal edges to prevent the occupant falling out during rough weather. Washing was done at the compactum which was filled with hot water provided by the cabin steward.

ORIENT LINE. S.S. "OMRAH".
Twin Screw, 8291 Tons reg 10,000 Horse Power.
PASSENGER CABIN.

ORIENT LINE S.S. "OMRAH".
Twin Screw, 8291 Tons reg 10,000 Horse Power.
DINING SALOON.

Many late nineteenth century ships had the drawing and smoking rooms radiating off the central well of the dining saloon. On *Omrah* these were situated on the promenade deck. The drawing room featured panels of silkwood and rosewood and a grand piano. On the right are angled panels covering the raked foremast which rose through this chamber.

Whilst the drawing room was carpeted, that male bastion, the smoking room, had wooden floors and oak panelling. The room was divided into a number of 'cosy corners' with seats covered in pigskin. A bar and lavatory were also nearby.

In contrast with that in first class, the second saloon was a very plain affair on the main deck with low ceilings of exposed steel and rivets, thin columns and the mainmast rising through the centre of the saloon. *[All Peter Newall collection]*

159

A VOYAGE WITH THE MAILS

(1864)   OFFICERS MUSTERING A BOATS' CREW.

VIEW ALONG THE BOAT DECK WHEN THE CREW GO TO BOAT STATIONS.   (K—113)

"BOAT STATIONS"—OFFICERS GOING TO REPORT TO THE COMMANDER ON THE BRIDGE.
(S—71)

FIRE STATIONS—A LINE OF "BLANKET MEN."   (0743)

THE "CAPTAIN COOK" LIFEBOAT IS LOWERED AND THE PILOT FERRIED ACROSS
(0817)   THE MAN SHOWING ON THE LINER IS HEAVING THE LEAD.

THE PILOT GETS ON BOARD BY CLIMBING UP A ROPE LADDER.   (0818)

Between 1910 and 1914 Orient Line produced a souvenir book for passengers, 'A voyage with the mails'. This describes in great detail a voyage from Tilbury to Australia on an Orient liner, probably *Otranto* (1). As many of the photographs provide a unique insight into life aboard an Edwardian Orient liner, a number have been reproduced here showing lifeboat drill, the arrival of the pilot at Sydney, and sports activities.
[Peter Newall collection]

(02008) COCK-FIGHTING—MANŒUVERING FOR A LIFT.

COCK-FIGHTING—A FALL. (02006)

(2607) START OF MEN'S POTATO RACE.
[Each competitor carries a potato balanced in a spoon, between his teeth.]

MEN'S JOCKEY RACE. (02001)

(S—328) PILLOW FIGHTING ON THE SPAR—A BAD SHOT.

BLINDFOLD DRIVING THROUGH BOTTLES. (843)

SPORTS ON BOARD SHIP.

161

Orama (2)

The large liners of the early 1900s saw the introduction of siting the main public rooms on a single deck, usually just below the boat deck, with its long unbroken promenade space. The dining saloons, however, remained below on the main deck as this was thought to be the most comfortable part of the ship in rough weather. *Orama* (2) of 1924 was the first of the new post-war liners and the spacious first-class public rooms were decorated in a Greek-style with fluted columns and soft colours. Many of the cabins were single-berth and were fitted with a basin with cold running water only. All the illustrations here are for first class.

[All: Peter Newall collection]

Right: At the time *Orama* (2) had more single-berth cabins than any other liner.

Below: The main lounge on B deck was 100 feet long and could comfortably seat 250 passengers.

Top: The cream and blue reading and writing room was at the forward end of C deck.

Left: The dining saloon on F deck looked like a Greek temple with its ionic columns and frieze depicting the labours of Hercules.

Below left: The open expanse of the boat deck.

Below right: A two-berth cabin.

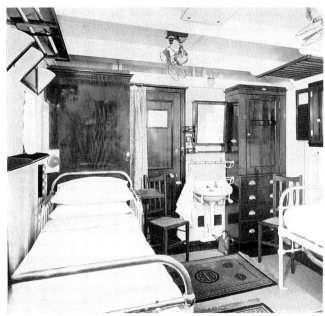

Orcades (2)

The hand-written brief given to Brian O'Rorke, the young New Zealand architect for the interior décor of the 1935 *Orion* and 1937 *Orcades* (2), stressed the need to escape from period decoration. Features such as fireplaces, wall-to-wall carpeting and curtains were only to be included if they had a real use – not merely for decoration. The result was a stunning set of public rooms which still look modern in the twenty-first century. *Orion* was also the first British liner to have air conditioning, although this was confined to the first class dining room. On *Orcades* (2) air conditioning was extended to a number of the best cabins and the first class library.

[*All: Peter Newall collection*]

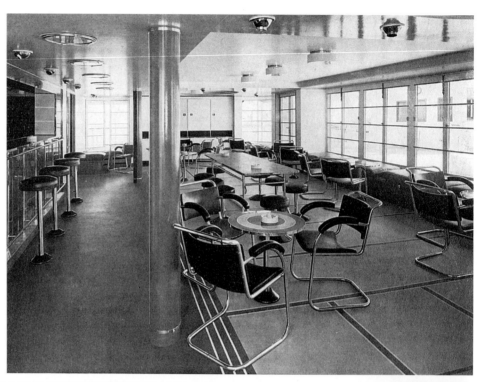

Right: The Tavern with its metal-framed chairs overlooked the swimming pool on C deck.

Below: The air-conditioned library was a delightful wood-panelled room with comfortable chairs and beautiful woven carpets.

Left: One of the special staterooms with private bathroom. Note the specially designed rugs and the sash windows in place of traditional portholes.

Below left: The uncluttered boat deck.

Below right: The swimming pool was protected from the elements by changing rooms on either side.

Empire Orwell: contrasts in accommodation

With a 1,000 passenger increase in her capacity, the former German liner *Pretoria* emerged in 1949 as the British troopship *Empire Orwell*. Interestingly, apart from furnishings, her two main first class public rooms on B deck remained little altered but her forward lower decks were transformed into high-density troop accommodation.

Above: The first class lounge was originally the first class social hall with its decorated dance floor and high glass doors opening onto an enclosed winter garden. The ceiling was floodlit from a bowl of chased bronze atop a single column situated at the centre of the room.

Below: Aft of the lounge was the smoking room panelled in dark woods. Curiously, the inlaid-wood map of Africa celebrating Germany's colonial past was left in situ because it 'portrayed Hitler's ambitions of world domination'. Given the amount of red on the maps of the time, this was a somewhat incongruous claim. *[National Maritime Museum: top G9033; bottom G9027]*

Above: The mess for the troops on E deck with long tables and fixed swivel chairs was almost a throw-back to second class dining on Orient ships of the nineteenth century.

Below: Four troop dormitories were situated forward of the engine rooms on F and G deck. Reaching the top bunks must have been quite a problem. For troops who misbehaved, there were six cells next to the chain locker in the peak of the bow.
[National Maritime Museum: top G9024; bottom G9023]

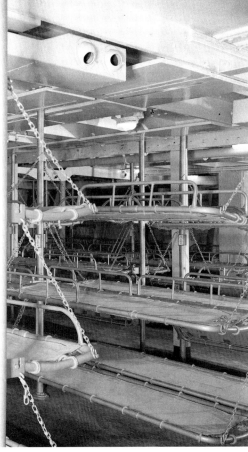

Oriana: the last of the line

Six months separated the delivery of *Oriana* and her larger P&O rival *Canberra* and although the latter won the hearts and minds of the British public, *Oriana* was the more advanced ship both inside and out. She certainly generated much negative and positive comment at the time but as Sir Colin Anderson, who had been in charge of Orient design since *Orion*, noted "The more you refuse to copy the past, the more criticism you get from that particular type of person. We have never believed in slavishly copying the last of our ships built but we are not looking for unusual design for the sake of originality". *Oriana* certainly reflected the modern and rather stark style of the time as the following photographs show.

Top right: Abstract low relief panel by Mary Martin in the first class stairwell.

Middle: The Princess Room, named after Princess Alexandra who launched *Oriana,* was one of the largest rooms in the ship. On the left was a large mural 'Landscape of the Two Seasons' by John Piper, which also screened the library. This painting is now in the P&O Art Collection.

Right: The first class ballroom continued a tradition on Orient ships going back to the 1920s.
[P&O Archives: top FT 86182-30; middle PO-1-5594; below PO-1-5592]

Top: Although the main first class restaurant was on E deck, there was also the Silver Grill on A deck for those who preferred more exclusive dining.

Above left: Specially designed crockery and silverware was part of the overall modern image of the ship.

Above right: The captain's night cabin. All passenger and crew areas were fully air-conditioned.

Right: The Spartan main tourist class entrance on E deck.

[P&O Archives: top FT 86283-8;
middle left FT 86182-27;
middle right PO-1-5863;
right PO-1-1644]

ORIENT LINE SURVIVALS
Oriana of 1960

It is a testament to the designers of *Oriana* that, seven years after the demolition of her P&O rival *Canberra*, she remained virtually intact as a visitor attraction in the Chinese city of Dalian, until June 2004 when she suffered storm damage. At the time of printing, her future remains uncertain with cranes stabilising her sharp list to port - lower photo.

Prior to that she flew the red flag of China on her stern and still keeps her original *Oriana* and 'London' stern lettering. Visitors to *Oriana* entered on D deck into a large lobby which occupies the full width of the ship and extends along much of the deck. This area was transformed in 2002 and has a section of glass flooring looking down into the engine room which, apart from the removal of two boilers, remains more or less unchanged.

Although her exterior, engine room and bridge have hardly altered, little exists of *Oriana*'s public rooms and passenger accommodation. Much of *Oriana*'s teak decking, however, remains including the forecastle which features two of her propellers and a rudder.

[All photos: Shane Spencer]

Orontes (1) of 1902

One of the most unusual items from an Orient liner can be found in Scotland at Aberdour on the north side of the Firth of Forth. Inside a comfortable country hotel, the Woodside Hotel, is the original barrel-vaulted roof from the 1902 *Orontes* (1). Not only is it in immaculate condition, its woodwork and colourful art nouveau stained glass is a perfect example of the quality of workmanship which was the hallmark of Orient Line.

Orontes (1) was broken up in 1925-1926 at nearby Inverkeithing and the roof bought by the owners of the nineteenth century hotel and installed in 1928 in what is now the Clipper Bar. Circular windows are a feature of the wood panelling and these still have their original openers, which allowed fresh air to circulate in hot weather. At either end are exquisitely carved coats of arms. The arms of Australia can be seen right and those of Great Britain below.

The stained glass is of particular interest as the ship was built at Glasgow where some of the finest art nouveau glass was made at the turn of the century. It also shows the influence of the Glasgow designer Charles Rennie Mackintosh and is unique because, at the time, British shipowners were very conservative and few would have used 'modern' glass design in their ships. *[Woodside Hotel]*

FLAGS, FUNNELS, LIVERY AND COAT OF ARMS

Anderson, Anderson and Co.
1869-1896
(This flag may have continued in use
on chartered ships. It was also used prior to 1869.)

The Orient Steam Navigation Co. Ltd.
1878-1880
(A combination of the flags of Anderson, Anderson
and Co. and Frederick Green and Co.)

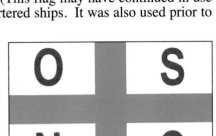

The Orient Steam Navigation Co. Ltd.

Pacific Steam Navigation Company

Orient Line Joint Service 1880-1888

The Orient Steam Navigation Co. Ltd.

Pacific Steam Navigation Company

Orient Line Joint Service 1888-1901
(Crown added when Australian mail service shared with P&O)

Orient-Pacific Line 1901-1906
(Initials dropped for both Orient and PSNC)
Orient-Royal Mail Line 1906-1909

Orient Steam Navigation Co. Ltd. 1909-1966

Funnel 1878-1906

Funnel 1906-1966
Introduced to conform with Royal Mail Line for
Orient-Royal Mail Line service.

HULLS

Black with red boot-topping until the arrival of *Orion* in 1935 when a corn-coloured hull with green boot-topping was introduced for all new ships. The pre-1935-built ships remained with black hulls and red boot-topping although at some stage the red boot-topping was replaced with green boot-topping.

In 1964 a new livery was introduced for all ships in the P&O-Orient Lines fleet: white hull; green boot-topping and yellow funnels. By the end of the 1960s the boot-topping reverted to red.

COAT OF ARMS

The motto of Orient Line was: **Par non leonina societas** – *An equal partnership with no lion's share* which could have applied to the partnership between Anderson, Anderson and Co. and Frederick Green and Co. and to that of The Orient Steam Navigation Co. Ltd. and Pacific Steam Navigation Co. It also referred to the relationship between Britain and Australia which is why the shield in the coat of arms features kangaroo and lion supporters. The company coat of arms and those of Britain and Australia were used in a number of the early ships whilst the first mentioned also appeared extensively in promotional material in the 1920s and 1930s (left hand crest). The Orient Line coat of arms (right) was officially granted by the College of Heralds, London on the 7th June 1957, three months before *Oriana's* keel was laid. Note the Anderson, Anderson and Co. flag on the mainmast of the sailing ship.

ORIENT LINE CRUISES
NORWAY & NORTHERN CAPITALS
20,000 TON STEAMERS

Managers:- ANDERSON, GREEN & Cº Lᵀᴰ. 5, Fenchurch Avenue, London, E.C.3.(Telephone MONUMENT 3456)
West End Offices:- 14, Cockspur Street, S.W.1.(Telephone GERRARD.9074) — 1, Australia House, Strand, W.C.2.(Telephone.CITY.5127)

CRUISING WITH ORIENT

Orient Line was one of the first shipping companies to operate cruise ships. From 1889 it offered cruises to the Norway and the Mediterranean in the summer months. Its promotional material was also very colourful and innovative. Here is a selection from 1907 to 1937.

[Left: Peter Newall collection; right and opposite page: Paul Louden-Brown collection]

PLEASURE CRUISES
BY Orient Cº Steamers
1907

ORIENT LINE
CRUISES 1937

Agents :
THOS. COOK & SON LTD.

HERBERT K. ROOKE

ORIENT LINE CRUISES

TO

MEDITERRANEAN, PALESTINE, EGYPT, GREECE, DALMATIAN COAST TOWNS, CANARY ISLANDS, Etc.

Write for Programme of Spring Cruises:

Managers ANDERSON, GREEN & Cº LTP 5, Fenchurch Avenue, London, E.C.3. Telegrams "ANDERSONS,FEN,LONDON" Telephone Nº CITY.3000.
West End Offices. 14, Cockspur Street, S.W.1. (Tel.No. GERRARD 9074.) 1, Australia House,Strand,W.C.2.(Tel.No CITY 5127.)

By S.S. "OTRANTO" & S.S. "ORFORD", 20,000 Tons

WINTER SUNSHINE

BY ORIENT LINE

WEST INDIES CRUISE

JANUARY 27–42 DAYS FROM 85 GUINEAS

SPECIAL FIRST-CLASS RETURN TICKETS TO

COLOMBO £105   EGYPT £60

Managers: Anderson, Green & Co., Ltd., 5 Fenchurch Avenue, London, E.C.3
West End Offices: 14 Cockspur Street, S.W.1, & No. I Australia House, Strand, W.C.2

ORIENT SHIPS IN COLOUR

Orient (2) passing Gibraltar. By R.H. Neville Cumming (1843-1920), signed and dated 1886.
[Courtesy of The British Mercantile Marine Memorial Collection]

Orsova (1) departing Sydney Heads. By John C. Allcot (1888-1973), signed and dated 1921.
[Courtesy of The British Mercantile Marine Memorial Collection.]

Passenger tender at Toulon flying the Orient Line house flag. At some stage before the First World War Orient switched calls in both directions from Marseilles to Toulon. The company reverted to Marseilles circa 1950 for homeward calls only. *[J. and M. Clarkson]*

The last of the 20,000-tonners *Orontes* (2) leaving Cape Town in 1961. The following year she was sold to Spanish breakers. *[Ian Shiffman]*

Two views of *Orion*. [Above: V. H. Young and L.A. Sawyer collection; below: World Ship Photo Library 31847]

Above: *Orcades* (3) at Malta. *[P&O Archives]*

Left and below: *Oronsay* (2) in P&O colours. The post-war Orient liners lost much of their uniqueness when they were painted all white. *[Both: V.H. Young and L.A. Sawyer collection]*

The handsome *Orsova* (2)   *[Both: P&O Archives]*

Oriana, launched on 3rd November 1959
(right) and in service (below).

[All: P&O Archives]

Three of the ships operated by the P&O Bulk Shipping Division and registered in the ownership of Orient Steam Navigation Co. Ltd. The liquified gas carriers *Garmula* (top) and *Garala* (left) and the ore/oil carrier *Lauderdale* (bottom).
[All: Fotoflite incorporating Skyfotos]

INDEX

All ships mentioned are listed. Names in capitals are those carried whilst in Orient ownership, the joint service, or management. Page numbers of fleet list entries are in bold type.

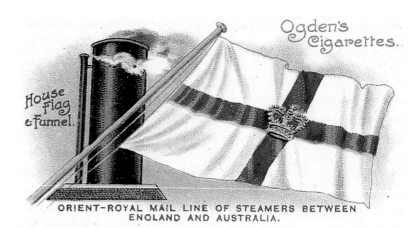

HIGNETT'S CIGARETTES.

ORIENT STEAM NAV. CO. LD.

Ogden's Cigarettes.

House Flag & Funnel.

ORIENT-ROYAL MAIL LINE OF STEAMERS BETWEEN ENGLAND AND AUSTRALIA.

Cigarette cards issued by Ogdens and Hignetts depicting the flags and funnel colours of Orient-Royal Mail and Orient, and Waddingtons' patience cards produced for Orient Line.

[Paul Louden-Brown collection and Heather Fenton collection]

On 30th September 1966 the Orient Line Commodore's flag was lowered for the final time by Commodore J.L. Dunkley aboard *Oriana*.

[P&O Archives]

184